MONEY IN MU$IC

EVERYTHING A MUSICIAN NEEDS TO KNOW TO
BECOME STEADILY EMPLOYED AS
A LIVE PERFORMER

BY CRAIG WARREN COLLEY

Edited by Neville L. Johnson, Esq. and Andrea Reeder. Editing contributions by Gloria Winship, Collette Blue, Robin Johnson, Sara Schindler, Shawn Edwards, Reed Colley, and Sarah Houston

Houston
PUBLISHING, INC.
224 SOUTH LEBANON STREET, LEBANON, IN 46052 U.S.A.

i

ISBN 1-56516-000-2

Library of Congress Catalog Card Number 91-73514

Houston
PUBLISHING,   INC.
224 SOUTH LEBANON STREET, LEBANON, IN 46052 U.S.A.

Contents

INTRODUCTION

This book has been written for musicians who wish to perform in the nightclub circuit, as well as for private parties, weddings, etc., in order to establish themselves as professionals in the music/entertainment industry. It provides information, suggestions and guidelines which should enable the skilled musician to become steadily employed as a performer.

Best of luck to you!

Craig Warren Colley

Many thanks to Robin, Collette, Neville, Andrea, Gloria, Reed, Sara, Shawn, Pat, Robyn & Jim, Vicky & Jim, *(these are two different Jim's by the way)*, Johnny & Collette, Oliver, Nancy & Sunny, Judy, Barb & Don, the 'Doc', Carol, Jenifer, Les, Muzzy, Missy and Laurel for helping me with this book. A *Special Thanks* to all the people who have hired me through the years to play for them and the people in my audiences who have supported my career.

ABOUT THE AUTHOR

Craig Warren Colley (aka Eddie Kidd) has been one of the most successful and highly paid entertainers in Southern California for many years. After having majored in Music in College, he toured coast-to-coast with some of the biggest show bands in the nation. A Songwriter and Producer with four independent records to his credit, he also sings and plays six instruments. He knows, and reveals, organizes and addresses the various challenges a professional performing musician must face. You will be able to fashion your own song list and material and plan sets from the guidelines provided.

CHAPTER ONE
GOALS

In the entertainment business, everyone wants to become a star, a recording artist or a performer. While not everyone makes it to stardom, those who do have made it there through very hard work. Whatever your own personal objective may be - nightclub entertainer, top recording musician, a star on Broadway, or a touring or recording artist - a realistic goal will get you through the tedious times and encourage you toward success.

You should have short-range goals, mid-range goals and long-range goals. Prepare an agenda which shows each goal in a step-by-step progression. Each small goal that you achieve will give you a sense of accomplishment and motivate you to continue. *Believe in yourself*; have confidence in your ability to achieve, even in the highly competitive, cut-throat and unpredictable business of entertainment.

Be patient, and remember that this is an *emotional* business. Often there will be conflict between your feelings as a musician/artist and your position as a business person. Realistic goals will help you achieve success and will set the direction and tone of your business methodology. *Wasted time is progress lost.* Do not miss any opportunities that arise for people to see and hear you. Be serious, objective and disciplined about adhering to your goals. As an accomplished musician and entertainer, you will be one of the most sensitive, desirable and sought-after people on earth!

CHAPTER TWO
PROMOTION

Good promotion of yourself is vitally important throughout your entire career. It will make or break you!

While climbing the ladder of success to accomplish your goals, remember that it takes time and you will go through many small steps. What you achieve is entirely up to you through your drive, self-discipline and willingness to grow. You'll need an organized and thorough plan.

Begin by developing your talent and repertoire. Decide what kind of bookings you are looking for, never overrating your current abilities. You will need a Promo Kit, as described below:

A **PROMO KIT** should contain the following items:

- *Stationery*

- *Photographs*

- *Bio/Resume*

- *Song List*

- *Promo or Demo Tape*

- *Video Tape (optional)*

- *Logo*

- *Business Cards*

- *Reviews or Classified Ads*

Stationery

Your letterhead stationery should be 8-1/2" x 11" and you can use a No. 10 business-size envelope. A larger 9" x 12" envelope can also be used to contain more materials, i.e. pictures, tapes, etc..Have your name, address and phone number professionally type-set. Choose high-quality paper materials such as linens, etc. Most local print shops carry what you need.

All promo materials should be designed and printed uniformly and in an eye-catching manner. The use of a **Logo** (see Logo on Page 7) on your stationery can be most advantageous. Be original and strive for perfection in your design and print. It will put you a step ahead of other applicants for the job.

Photographs

Black and white 8" X 10" photos of yourself are fine. Have your pictures taken by a professional photographer who specializes in creating photographs which will portray you in an interesting and flattering manner.

Avoid portrait studios. This is not a picture for a high school yearbook or your mother's bedroom wall. Photographs may be taken indoors or outside, but the main focus must be on you and not your surroundings or background.

Your photo should say something about you and display your best features. If your picture is to be half-toned, insist that it reproduce clearly. *(A half-tone is a dot pattern applied to a photo; this must be done prior to printing on paper or in a newspaper or magazine).* As long as the photo is not drastically different from the way you look in person, I encourage touching up or airbrushing to bring out your best. Head shots are the most desirable for a solo act, followed by waist-up portraits. Because of half-tone reproduction, duos and trios, or larger groups should project their faces and not do full-body shots.

In most advertisements, your photo will be reduced in size to fit an ad space. For multiple copies, have your promo shot reproduced by a quality printer which is more economical than having 8" X 10" glossy photos made. To find referrals for an excellent photographer, contact local modeling agencies. For basic printing needs, check your local phone book. Be sure you and your photographer provide a space on your photo for your name, address and telephone number or the name and telephone number of your agent.

Bio/Resume

All information should be informative, but brief and on one page. Describe yourself and your music, emphasizing your strengths and using as few words as possible.

1. *List your musical education,*

2. *Highlight your performance history,*

3. *Describe your on-stage musical capabilities, and*

4. *Specify whether you compose your own music and what your goals are.*

Each section should be separate and brief. <u>Underline</u> and use **BOLD** or *italic* font to emphasize the most pertinent information. If possible, mention that references and past places of performance, videos and other promotional materials are available upon request.

Song List

Categorize your songs under different headings. For example, Ballads, AC (Adult Contemporary) or MOR (Middle of the Road), 50's, 60's, 70's, 80's or 90's and Variety (city, novelty, show, old standards, etc.).* Remember, the more songs creatively arranged and/or stylized that you can play, the more diversified gigs you'll be able to obtain and perform.

---

*For more Song List info, see Chapter 22 for examples.

Promo or Demo Tape

Strive for the best possible recording you can afford. The recording should represent what you are and what you sound like "live". Use a variety of song styles, to show your versatility but have no more than four on the tape. Another alternative is to put together a medley of songs that display your different styles of music.   You must play a variety of songs in club work. Some will be right for you, some will not. Unfortunately, you have to sing them all, but put only your best work on the tape. Make cassettes for promo use and distribution. Use the finest quality tape and duplication process your budget allows. Purchase cassette labels (available from most stationery shops or printing supply stores) and either type or have printed on them your name or that of your band. Also include the songs on the tape and most importantly your phone number or that of your agent.

Video Tape

Unless you can afford to hire at least a semi-professional video production company, I advise against video for promotion. Do not use home shot videos for promo unless they are exceptionally well done.

In video, you are competing with a professional medium everyone is used to seeing. Anything less than "air quality" footage looks inferior compared to the standardized expectation we're accustomed to. Most of the time, a "home video" will do more harm than good. Remember, it's better to show a few good things about your act than anything mediocre. Again, label it with your name, the songs and a phone number.

Logo

If you choose to have a logo, it can be simple typography or you can have a logo created for you by hiring a commercial artist. A logo can be very useful because it will be remembered, associated, and identified only with you

Here is an example of two of mine:

Personal Logo
(done by a commercial artist)

Company Logo
(Computer generated graphics)

Business Cards

Your business card should have your name and phone number clearly printed on it. This is another place to incorporate a logo if you have one. Any print shop can help with the design. If you want to include an address, I strongly recommend using a PO Box number and not your home address.

This is an example of my business card:

Some Final Notes:

1. Include in your promo kit duplicate copies (always keep the originals) of any advertisements, reviews or write-ups about you, along with listings from entertainment sections of local newspapers which mention you or your band.

2. Use a post office box number for your return address on your stationery, envelopes, mail cards and business cards. This will help protect your privacy and keep weirdos away.

3. Your Promotion can be marketed in concession form as well to sell at your shows. This can serve a dual purpose: One to advertise you and the other to generate extra income.

If you follow the above suggestions, you will make a professional presentation and establish a professional image which will place you at the forefront of your field!

CHAPTER THREE
AGENTS

The booking agent plays a very important role in the career of any musician/entertainer because his main job is to find employment - or, in the music business - "gigs".

Your agent negotiates and oversees all business transactions involving you as a performer including contracts, the rate at which your employer is to pay you, and the times and dates of engagements and auditions. Make available to him your **Promo Kit** which, of course, will contain pertinent information relating to you, your talents and your availability to perform or audition. Some agents require an audition exclusively for them so they can first judge whether they can book you.

Never pay an agent money up front; work only on a commission basis. Standard commission fees range from ten percent to twenty percent, depending on the circumstances of your particular engagement; in most cases, booking agents earn fifteen percent. You and your agent should agree on a commission prior to your first gig to avoid complications that may arise later. If you are not booked properly and are unsuccessful financially, your agent likewise suffers.

It is important to remember that your agent is working for you. Don't be intimidated. The agent secures the engagements, you do the performing. Most agents specialize in certain fields, so you should work with one who primarily books acts in your genre. He or she will know the available nightclubs or private parties that are seeking your type of entertainment. In return, you must behave like a professional and be punctual, cordial and reliable for all meetings and gigs.

Some agents require the signing of either their own or a union-designed contract before they will represent you. My recommendation is to *"execute"* (legalese for "sign") *only non-exclusive contracts*. This means you can be booked by other agents as well. It is always wise to put any agreement in writing to avoid future disagreements.

To find an agent:

1. Seek references from other musicians or your local music union.

2. Contact nightclubs to find out what agent represents their bookings.

3. Study the trade publications listing agents.

4. Examine the phone book and the Yellow Pages.

You must be cordial, polite, ambitious and respectful at all times when working with your agent. Present yourself as a knowledgeable, self-confident person who is focused on one goal - attaining a successful career through good bookings. Be thoughtful; an agent's job is hard work. Establish a good business relationship with him or her. Send a small gift and/or thank you card after you receive confirmation of a successful booking.

An agent's main interest is making money through your success and talents. Initially, the agent may go to great lengths to secure you a booking and seem completely involved in your career. However, don't be surprised if once you are working steadily, you seldom see or hear from him or her unless you are late on a commission payment. After all, the agent's only responsibility is to find gigs for you.

If you are engaged in any long-term work, try to arrange an open-ended contract with a two-week escape or ending clause. A two week escape or ending clause declares that when you decide to move to another gig or booking you are contracted to give a two week notice so they (the person or club where you are presently working) can find someone to replace you. This also means the person or establishment that hired you is in turn contracted to give you a two week notice if they no longer want you to work for them. It is suggested that you plan a de-escalating commission scale to commence after a certain period of time. For example, if an agent books you for fifteen percent of your pay, after six months (and you are playing the exact same gig), the commission could be reduced to ten percent; after nine months to seven percent; and after twelve months to five percent. Why? Your agent's work is completed after you are initially booked. So basically, if there has been no change in the days or nights you work, the hours you play or the pay you make, your agent has been collecting commissions while just sitting idle. Still it's really up to you to keep your agent involved. Call him or her frequently to keep a good rapport and insist they come to see you perform as often as possible. *If you don't, they won't.*

In the event that friction develops between you and your agent, handle it with tact and diplomacy. There may come a time when you need that agent again. Remember that many agents are, or have been musicians themselves and know the "ins and outs" of the business. They can be helpful in coaching you and strengthening your abilities - which will help both of you to prosper.

With experience, you will learn the tricks-of-the-trade and, if you choose, you can manage your own bookings. If you do, always conduct yourself in a professional and business-like manner when dealing with a prospective employer.

CHAPTER FOUR
EQUIPMENT

Your equipment consists of your instrument(s), sound and lighting systems. They are your tools of the trade. How you choose to amplify and light yourself, as well as your choice of instruments, is your responsibility.

When purchasing any instrument, be thorough. Know what you are buying. It must be one of good quality in tone and resonance, and include a durable and road worthy case. New instruments are ideal, of course, but good deals on used ones are always available, often for bargain prices. Try and purchase only name-brand products so that your warranties will be valid when service is needed. <u>Believe me, from time-to-time it will be needed</u>. Always be prepared with extra parts such as strings, cords and any necessary repair tools. Take care of your instrument and keep it as visually attractive as possible. If you are an acoustic piano player, a piano will usually be provided where you will be performing, but carry with you your own tools for some occasional touch-up tunings, such as a tuning arm and some rubber wedges. If you have a steady gig playing a particular piano, installing some damp chasers or heat bars (with a humidistat), which keep temperatures constant for the instrument, can help to keep it in tune. These are particularly useful if you perform somewhere near water like a cruise ship, a lake or an ocean. Contact your local music store or piano technician for details regarding this.

Sound Systems

Although some nightclubs provide sound systems, it's a good idea to be equipped with your own. Musicians' needs will be different from one to another, but basically, you want to get a sound system which is reliable, easy to move and - most important - a brand that can be serviced easily.

I recommend a stereo system, using one channel for your main output and the other channel for your monitors (speakers projected toward the musician so you can hear yourself). This will enable you to hear the same volume levels of your voice(s), instrument(s), and outboard effects heard by your audience. A P.A. system can be made as basic or as sophisticated as you want it, and the technology available from which you can select is incredible! There is an almost endless array of cabinets, crossovers, power amplifiers, eq's, mixing consoles and effects. Go for a high quality sound with enough power to amplify without distortion and one built for the road.

A new system with a guarantee protecting you is the best to purchase, but you can find high quality used gear on the market. Some music stores sell used merchandise, but the best bet is to buy from your local music trade or newspaper classified ads. "For sale" cards posted on bulletin boards of music stores have proven to be another successful resource.

Check and double check the equipment you purchase to be sure it is functioning perfectly. Bring a friend with you who knows about equipment if you don't. The cosmetics or looks of the system are secondary to its performance and features. Use top grade cords and cables, and keep them in good condition so they will last. Something as simple as a bad cord or connection can keep your system from functioning properly.

Microphones and Pickups

Transmitting your voice or instrument through a sound system requires a microphone and a pickup. Become well-informed through inquiries at your local music store as to which one is best suited for your needs. Your product selection should be intended for live applications which can stand the abuse of steady work and regular travel. A delicate microphone may sound better, but once dropped, it may be irreparable. If you use an acoustic instrument, there are several types of pickups that can be applied for sound reproduction. Consult your local music dealer for information in aiding you to make the choice that is proper for your standards.

Lighting

Most nightclubs provide some kind of lighting. This may not concern you now, but as your career progresses, lighting will become more important and essential to your show. Lighting can accent, emphasize and accentuate moods in your music and add special effects and dimensions to your show. Contact sound and lighting companies; get to know lighting men and ask for their recommendations.

Be prepared!

Have extra fuses, cables, cords, strings, microphones, etc., in case of emergencies.

Remember, this is no one's responsibility but your own.

CHAPTER FIVE

REHEARSALS

Rehearsals fall into three categories:

1. The selection and continually disciplined practice of the material to be performed in your nightclub routine;

2. Updating your current shows with additional, newly learned material; and

3. Rehearsing songs that need improvement.

To be more specific: In selecting material, find songs that fit your style, instrumental ability, vocal range and performance format. Initially, you will need at least fifty songs from which you can derive enough material to provide at least one full evening of entertainment. Not only must your beginning rehearsals prepare you musically, but they must also enable you to train your voice to sing four or five nights in a row, every week, without burning it out. You must work up to this level gradually through daily practice - an hour the first day, an hour and a half the second day, two hours the third day, etc. Never push or overexert yourself. Be prepared, voice-wise, before you begin a new gig on a regular basis. Your voice must be ready to undertake the pressure and strain of live performing.

Use any and all means of finding and learning new songs including sheet music, fake books, lyric sheets of albums, and by ear. Add to your repertoire as many different songs as possible; you can then cover a wide range of requests received during a night's performance. Arrange familiar medleys of certain eras of music and songs by the same artist.

Transposing - *changing a song from its original key to a different key - is a technique you need to develop. While transposing can be tricky, it may be necessary so that a song can be made to fit your voice. The following is a simple and brief description of how to do it.*

Example: *For piano or keyboard:*If a song is written in the key of E, but that key is too high for you to sing in, try changing it to D or C. Change all chords in the song down or up, whatever the case may be, to the same interval (the difference in pitch between two tones). For example, if the song is in the key of G, change the chords G, C , and D down two intervals to F, B-flat, and C. Now the song is changed to the key of F. Thus, you can sing the song a whole step down.

The following are a few common transpositions down to a lower key.

Original Key → **DOWN** - 1 key	2 keys	3 keys	4 keys	5 keys	6 keys	7 keys
C — B	B♭/A♯	A	A♭/G♯	G	G♭/F♯	F
D — D♭/C♯	C	B	B♭/A♯	A	A♭/G♯	G
E — E♭/D♯	D	D♭/C♯	C	B	B♭/A♯	A
F — E	E♭/D♯	D	D♭/C♯	C	B	B♭/A♯
G — G♭/F♯	F	E	E♭/D♯	D	D♭/C♯	C
A — A♭/G♯	G	G♭/F♯	F	E	E♭/D♯	D
B — B♭/A♯	A	B♭/G♯	G	G♭/F♯	F	E

The following are a few common transpositions up to a higher key.

Original Key → UP -	1 key	2 keys	3 keys	4 keys	5 keys	6 keys	7 keys
C	C♯/D♭	D	D♯/E♭	E	F	F♯/G♭	G
D	D♯/E♭	E	F	F♯/G♭	G	G#/A♭	A
E	F	F♯/G♭	G	G♯/A♭	A	A♯/B♭	B
F	F♯/G♭	G	G♯/A♭	A	A♯/B♭	B	C
G	G♯/A♭	A	A♯/B♭	B	C	C♯/D♭	D
A	A♯/B♭	B	C	C♯/D♭	D	D♯/E♭	E
B	C	C♯/D♭	D	D♯/E♭	E	F	F♯/G♭

Naturally, if you transpose select a comfortable key - one that suits your voice.   Because of the large number of songs that you must sing during a given night, you must protect your voice; transposing will help you to perform in your best key.

For guitar: If you are a guitarist and most of the songs you sing are just a little too high for your vocal range, one alternative to transposing is to use a heavy gauge set of strings and tuning the guitar a half or whole step or key down. This enables you to play the standard open chords and still have a full, rich-sounding guitar while singing in a lower key.

You can also purchase a *cappo* from any music store. This device is placed in between any two frets and wraps around the neck of your guitar and fastens tightly. Depending where it is placed, all the chords you play normally will now be transposed up into a different key.

For example: If you play an E chord with the cappo on 3rd fret up, it will sound like a G chord. Experiment for yourself. On guitar, some songs sound better if you use a cappo. You can actually change the chords and still remain in the same original key you started. For example: If you place the cappo on the 4th fret up and play a C chord, it will really be an E chord. It just sounds different because of the voicing of the chord. Try it and see.

After you have learned most of your material, prepare a scratch song or play list for your sets. In solo, duo, and even trio work, you don't need to confine yourself to a strict play list, but it is always advisable to have one for reference so as to eliminate dead spots in your shows.

Throughout your entertainment career, you must constantly learn new songs, be they old or contemporary. Doing so will keep you from growing stale to the crowd and to yourself, and it's especially important if you play in one club for a lengthy period of time. Consider using a "Song Request/Suggestion Box" for ideas or leave a space on your mail list cards, table tents or in your mailing list book for requests.* Choose the best-loved old songs that are heavily requested and which will have staying power. Many current Top 40 songs are in demand only for a short period. Because radio stations saturate their play list with repetition of hit songs, people become tired of them and often do not want to hear them in a nightclub act after they have lost their initial popularity. You will find that some songs work out great in rehearsal, but not in live performance. Don't be disillusioned by this; just realize that the way a crowd feels and the way you feel about a song can be entirely different.

* For more info on Mail Cards and Books, see Chapter 17 , Page 39

Understand that your job is to please the crowd, not yourself. Through experience, I have discovered that for every ten songs I master, five of them will be used consistently and the other five will be cut from the show because they did not elicit a strong positive reaction from the crowd. Even if you don't use every song you learn, you will always have it in your repertoire and will probably have opportunity to use it at some point. Moreover, you learn from experience what a live audience demands. When introducing a new song into your format, it must be well rehearsed and as polished as everything else that you do. Your level of professionalism, style and talent must be consistently superior.

Make mental notes during your nightly sets of the songs in which you make mistakes or with which you have vocal problems; then, during your break, jot down a note as a reminder to rehearse them again before your next performance. A better way to catch your mistakes is to have a micro cassette recorder with you on stage. In between songs, you can whisper into it what you need to remember. By consistently doing this, you will achieve the standard of excellence needed to establish yourself as a quality performer. You do not want your audience or your employer to perceive or foresee any weaknesses in your talent or capabilities. *Let them see only your strengths!*

It is all in your hands. How badly do you want it?

You can reach your goal . . .

IT'S ALL UP TO YOU!

CHAPTER SIX
AUDITIONS

Auditioning in the music business is simply a job interview where your qualifications and talents are critiqued. Most gigs require an audition. As a newcomer in the business, you will need to be seen and heard by someone looking for an act to book, whether for private parties or nightclub engagements. Your agent, if you have one, will inform you of the time, place, location, type of music to perform and the proper attire. The arrangements made and the particular circumstances of any audition vary widely, so be prepared to expect the unexpected. It is always wise to learn as much as you can about the audition on your own because sometimes an agent will not have accurate information.

Be on time, well prepared and ready to knock 'em dead! Don't become discouraged if you do not get every job that you have auditioned for, because it doesn't happen that way. It's kind of like baseball; if you don't connect with your first pitch, you keep swinging until you get a hit. Even if you have a "killer" promo video tape, you'll probably still have to audition. Once you're established, your auditions will be infrequent because you will then be able to book yourself based on your track record.

Always carry your **Promo Kit** with you. Appear confident and knowledgeable, and be courteous and gracious. It's normal to feel nervous at first; your nervousness will disappear after you've done a few auditions. With experience, you will become a real pro and find that the payoff is well worth the effort.

CHAPTER SEVEN
SETS AND PLAY LISTS

Your music should be a mixture of new songs and an abundance of the older hits. Capture the melodies, as opposed to the original recorded sound or arrangement of the songs. Gear your set list and personality according to the type of situation or room set-up in which you are working. Be prepared.

Play the longest sets early in the evening. In single's or duos' rooms, you will frequently play to an "early" crowd. Use contests, gimmicks and the like for the third show to keep the crowd with you. Announce what is coming up throughout your performance.

Starting the Night:

A. Open with a contemporary song (preferably AC/MOR; see Song List in Chapter 22, Page 52) that is well-liked and recognizable. If the introduction of the song is suitable, you can introduce yourself or your band over the top of the music before you begin to sing.

B. Comment about applause. If applause is good, compliment the crowd, such as:

- *"We've got a good crowd here tonight."*

- *.."That's the way to start it out."*

- *..A very humble "thank you" to let them know how much you appreciate their response.*

C. If the applause is so-so or none at all, say:

• .."It's OK to clap, if you like."

• .."Hey, this isn't a video, this is a live show now - it's OK to clap."

• ..If only a few people clap you can say, "That's the way to start out. Maybe it will catch on and spread through the room."

• .."You guys have only two jobs tonight - to have fun and to clap your hands when the song is over."

First Show

Begin with a few easy songs to warm up your voice and fingers. After two to four songs, start asking for requests. The first show is generally aimed at a dinner crowd who usually are not ready to party at that hour. Ballads, AC/MOR, and easy C&W are appropriate. Finish with a couple of exciting show stoppers.

Save certain songs for the "right time". If requested early, explain briefly and tactfully that there is a strategy to this job, and you will do them when the time is right.

Second and Third Shows

Start with an upbeat, but not overpowering song which allows for an intro in which you should again introduce yourself. Announce your intentions. For example, when asking for requests, tell the audience that you're going to get the place rockin', partyin', motivated, etc., and that you will be doing sing-alongs and contests. Sense the emotions of your crowd. If they are rowdy, make your music correspond with their mood. But pace yourself. Save your top song material for the time when your audience and momentum of the show are peaking. When you roll, all song requests performed must be fast and lively. Even accompanied by a substantial tip, the wrong song request can kill the momentum of your set. *(Unless it's a hundred dollar bill - just kidding).* Your repertoire should have variety, pleasing everyone with music that they know and like. Gradually work up to your finale. Choose a familiar song with a good tempo - which permits audience participation. This will encourage encores.

If you perform original songs, play them sparingly and at times when the crowd will listen and accept them. If you are a good songwriter, by all means take advantage of any gig to showcase your music. Just remember that any song that is unfamiliar - whether it's your own or someone else's - may cause the crowd's attention to drift away from you and your performance. *In some rare cases, you won't be allowed to do your originals. A gig at Disneyland is a good example of this.*

NOTE: Please refer to the song lists and description sections (Chapters 21, 22 and 23) for reference when planning your sets.

CHAPTER EIGHT
ATTITUDE

Your daily attitude about yourself, your music, your clientele, business associates and employer must always be positive. Don't let a negative attitude cost you. Too many times musicians think they are doing the club a favor by playing there; however, the opposite is true. Be thankful the club has hired you, because if they hadn't, you wouldn't have a place to perform your music, exercise your talent, and move toward your life goals.

Develop a logical, functioning business mind. This includes always being Mr. Nice Guy, while at the same time taking a practical view of what works and what doesn't work in the light of available time and resources. Sometimes you will have to bite your tongue and swallow your pride, even when you think you shouldn't have to. You may not always be treated with respect by waiters, waitresses, bartenders and managers; they may be jealous of the way you earn your paycheck. Avoid getting a "big head." Remain optimistic and positive. Adversity is part of the challenge of being a great performer.

CHAPTER NINE

PERSONALITY

Be full of life!

You must seem carefree, happy and fun to be around.

You must project that you are on top of the world.

You must keep up with the latest fads and current events.

You must seem to have the world in the palm of your hands.

You must have PERSONALITY!

In the music business, and especially in nightclub work, a strong and attractive personality is essential. It may be difficult at the start of your career to be extremely personable, because you will find yourself fighting all the problems inherent to slow or off-night gigs (usually Sundays, Mondays, and Tuesdays). Know your "enemy"; be prepared with a good routine and a tremendous musical repertoire. You can't be shy or insecure. Think about and study the personalities of people you admire and to whom you relate. Incorporate some of their characteristics. You don't have to change the way you are in your everyday life, but to some extent you are an actor or actress when under the spotlight. Without becoming a phony or someone that you really are not, you will want to enhance and strengthen every part of yourself without fear of trying new ideas. Comedians, talk show hosts, DJ's, video jocks or VJ's, journalists, television magazine personalities, newscasters, sportscasters, and weathercasters are all people who can give you good ideas about what works and what doesn't work in a performance setting. Watch them carefully and use what they have to offer, then throw in ideas of your own until you come up with the style which works best for you.

Eye contact is an especially important tool for the stage or club performer. People want to know that you are relating to them. Look them "right in the eye". Your eyes can be used to speak for you when you sing or play; an expression can be amplified by suggestive *eye contact*, and by the same token, this carries the message that you are acknowledging your audience's existence and, when you speak with them, demonstrates your interest and concern about what you are saying and thinking. Through *eye contact* with your audience as you perform, you can bring the crowd together and help them feel special. Such is the name of the game: Making each member of your audience feel good.

CHAPTER TEN

IMAGE

Create a consistent image. People remember not only what you do, but who you are and what you look like. "Looks" include your style of makeup, hair, fashion, clothes, jewelry, cologne or perfume, and your grooming in general. You want to enhance and project your best features.

Your image and appearance must be decided upon before you begin your first job. Be different, but not too radical. If you are not required to wear a uniform or costume at every gig, your wardrobe should be extensive. For all auditions, present the appearance of a well-organized, attractively-clothed, gifted musician - a professional. Be cautious when you have your hairstyle changed or cut; don't make such major changes immediately before a gig takes place Allow a few days prior to the gig so that you have time to get used to the change and feel comfortable with it. One should never perform before a crowd feeling uncomfortable because of his/her appearance. For example, if you want a mustache or beard, grow it during a vacation break

People in show business set trends. The public expects entertainers and musicians to support the newest in dress - so do so. Stay on top of current, interesting and appealing styles. Be unusual and daring, but not ridiculous. Never take away from the "real you" and what makes you feel comfortable and good about yourself on stage. Trust your instincts.

CHAPTER ELEVEN

HEALTH, DRINKING AND DRUGS

It is most important that you are physically fit and mentally alert at all times. Like any independent contractor, if you are unable to work, you will not receive a paycheck. There are no sick days. Eat properly, especially on the road. Good eating habits prevent illness and fatigue. Get exercise and rest. Look the best you can.

Have a positive mental attitude. Of course, there are times when illness strikes, but you should first have it in your mind that no sickness is going to stop you from missing a gig. Find yourself a good doctor who understands your job and its rigors. Rely on him or her and follow the doctor's orders. Stay away from situations that jeopardize your health. Watch out for excessive partying or strenuous sports activities that may take away the physical strength you need for a night's performance. Be careful when working on or with equipment that could be hazardous to your hands and feet.

To have staying power in the music business, you must keep your youth as long as possible. You can do that by maintaining your health to the highest degree. There is no substitute for a healthy body and mind.

Alcohol and Drugs

The cultures, lifestyles and environments in the world today provide us with alcohol and drugs virtually everywhere we look. These substances are always available to entertainers and they can alter one's disposition, motivation and productivity. In fact, as a musician at a nightclub, you are in the paradoxical position of promoting the sale of alcohol to your audience in order to satisfy your employer, while at the same time needing to abstain from it yourself in order to be the best musician you can be.

The business of nightclubs is selling alcohol and you will find yourself constantly surrounded by drinkers and smokers. The effect of drinking and drugs varies from one individual to another, but one thing is certain: If you indulge in and rely on them, the more likely you are to compromise your professionalism and do real damage to your professional image. Don't complicate your life. Distracting yourself from your goals can be destructive to your health and talent, causing many more problems. You must always have full control over your faculties, mentally and physically, constantly being professional.

The music business is "dog eat dog", and you have to be better than the next person who comes along. However, don't worry about your competitors; just concentrate on being your best. The audience waits for you every night to bring out of them an array of emotions and feelings. The more you fulfill their desires, the more successful you will be. You are in a nightclub to sell alcohol. The dollar sign that rings on the cash register reflects how successful you have been as an entertainer in the eyes of your employer. When you get right down to it, if you or your band doesn't sell enough drinks, you don't have a job. On the other hand, you don't want to encourage anyone to get drunk. You are a citizen before you are a musician, and moreover, you are a potential defendant if someone you helped get drunk then causes injury to other people as a result of their intoxication. If you act responsibly, you'll always have a gig.

Having a good time and making people happy is what your work as a musician is all about. Compare the difference in your audience from your first song to your last. Generally, the more drinks people have had, the better they will respond. Utilize such situations to your advantage.

How you live your personal life is your business. Don't confuse it with the fact that playing music is your job. Stay straight!

CHAPTER TWELVE

YOUR WORK HABITS: PUNCTUALITY AND BREAKS

Punctuality

Being punctual is related to responsibility, especially in the entertainment business, as musicians and entertainers are stereotyped as being unreliable. Remove any doubt from a prospective agent or employer's mind that you are a risk. Since most nightclubs, hotels and lounges depend heavily on the entertainment for their success and stability, it is extremely important that you be on time for interviews, auditions and performances.

Purchase a good, reliable watch - if necessary, one with an alarm to help keep you on time. Always plan to reach your destination of work a half-hour ahead of schedule to ensure being on time. Bear in mind that you never know when traffic might delay you from keeping auditions or gigs.

Breaks

During your performance, you'll have scheduled breaks. In a nightclub situation, your breaks should be a time of rest between performances and a time to mingle with your clientele for promotional purposes. Make yourself known for your personable and likable attitude. If your audience admires and respects you both on and off stage, they will come back. Talk with as many people as possible during each break. People will be pleased in your efforts to meet them. You may meet agents or a person helpful to the advancement of your career. Show your appreciation of faithful followers by kind words or occasionally buying them a drink, but do so only if the club you're working in is allowing you some complimentary drinks to give away. It doesn't make sense to take money out of your pocket at the same time you're earning it.

Breaks should be part of a predictable routine for your audience and the club. Avoid leaving the premises during your breaks; because of the stereotypes that musicians seem to live with, some people might assume that if you leave the nightclub where you are working during your break, you are involved in the use of drugs. Most clubs which book small acts do not provide dressing rooms. Therefore, when you need to get away from everyone, use the restroom as your place of refuge; it is often the only place to be alone.

Make a habit of *checking your look in a mirror* every time before you return to the stage. Remember, your appearance and talent are both very important in how you present yourself to your audience.

CHAPTER THIRTEEN
AD LIBBING, GIMMICKS AND TIMING

Ad Libbing

Every performance provides an opportunity for a unique social gathering, and your ability to ad lib can add a great deal to the atmosphere. You can work your audience to its fullest potential, commenting on personalities, fashions , special events or responding to a comment made to you by a patron. Ad libs keep things fresh and exciting, while enhancing and broadening your personality and appeal to the audience.

Ad libbing can be a reflection of your own emotions. People go out to be entertained, so use, if you can, a strong asset - *comedy* - and make them laugh. You will help them to feel good "all over" and they will come back for more!

Gimmicks

Gimmicks work. They are attention seekers and tools to create a desired effect. They include such things as props (sunglasses, hats, changes of clothing, etc.) which are funny and make people laugh. Trivia, drinking or singing contests. also prove to be quite popular!

Remember that nightclub owners are most interested in the numbers rung up on their cash registers. Gimmicks can increase the size of your audience and the volume of liquor sales. If you can help toward this end, your employer will want to keep you around!

Timing

Good timing, pacing and the delivery of your routine are essential components of every performance. You will develop a "feel" for this based on what you perceive to be the audience's mood, temperament and interest on each given night. There will be nights when your clientele are in high spirits and there will be nights when they are depressed. Most nights, they will be somewhere in between these two extremes.

Your routine should be fairly similar night after night. As you perform and refine the songs, skits and one-liners, decide which ones work best for you. You will establish your own style and means of communicating with the audience and in the course of doing so, will discover which songs are popular and which are not. Certain songs will elicit the same reaction almost every time you play them; you can use these songs to establish a format that produces excellent results every night.

CHAPTER FOURTEEN

TIPPING

Tipping can be a major source of income for you if you handle it properly. If you don't mention anything about tips, they will remain minimal; so talk about it - but *tactfully* and with humor wherever possible.

On the following page are some examples:

•.."You can think of me as your own personal jukebox. Put money in the machine, and the machine plays your song."

•.."I've been doing a lot of songs on credit up here and haven't seen (much or any) money coming up, and your credit has just about run out."

•..After an encore, say "OK, now let's talk about the important part of all this. I've been up here a long time, and I haven't seen much money come up here (to keep me motivated to play)."

•..If there is no reply on tips, say "Hey, I can wait", and do just that. But, remember not to pause so long that the audience begins to get hostile toward you. Sometimes, people just won't tip.

•..When money starts flowing, encourage it with some humor. After one dollar comes up, say "Now we have part of a song." After another dollar, say "Now we have half of a song." After the third dollar comes, "Three-fourths of a song, we're almost there." During this process, you can add, "Can somebody finish this song?" and continue breaking each dollar coming up into small fractions, i.e. 7/8, 15/16, etc. The reaction from the audience usually is laughter.

•..If someone throws up small change, you can try saying "Oh a quarter, here's your note" and hit just one quick note on your instrument. That always gets a laugh.

•..Make jokes about why you need the money, such as, "I have bills to pay just like everyone else, and I want you to know that I spend this money on things I need to survive." Use ridiculous examples, such as "I have to tune up my Porsche," "I have to put a new paint job on my helicopter," "I have to re-carpet my yacht," and so on.

•.."Tipping is not a town in China" and "Remember, it's hip to tip" can also be used.

•..There are opportunities to be creative and witty and make money for yourself. It's a fact that people like other people who make them laugh!

•..Ask the crowd if they want to hear some more Rock & Roll, and then start playing the beginning four notes of "Old Time Rock & Roll". Then, stop and go into something like "Feelings". Encourage them to tip you so you'll play "Old Time Rock & Roll" again. You can repeat this routine again and go into another song like "Tie a Yellow Ribbon". Repeat this using different songs. It works great! (*Just be sure to eventually play the first song.*)

•..Acknowledge and compliment the generous tippers.

•..Put a toy basketball hoop on top of your tip jar and encourage the crowd to make "baskets" into it. Suggest that they roll up the bills into a ball and throw them in. When they miss, you can say, "Try a twenty - it goes right in!"

•..Be equipped with two or three good-sized tip jars. At the beginning of your performance, put a dollar of your own in one of the tip bowls to be used as bait, while holding back the other two jars. This will give the audience the idea that they should tip you for requests. As soon as one jar fills up, bring out another.

The above examples have worked for me again and again, and can work for you, too, along with any techniques of your own that you come up with!

CHAPTER FIFTEEN
HECKLERS AND JOB HAZARDS

Like weeds in a garden, there will be hecklers in your audience almost every time you perform. But don't worry - you can deal with them.

Heckling is usually a verbal expression of a person's mood or situation, and usually it comes out in the form of sarcasm.

In most situations, ignoring the heckler is the best approach.   You never have to acknowledge the existence of a rude person. Stay cool, even if it is tearing you apart inside. Never show that you are upset.

If you must say something in response, try to get the crowd on your side. Hold the cards in your hands. Use creative responses to outwit the hecklers and put them in their place. For example, you might comment on their most obvious and apparent physical weaknesses - but don't be cruel. Here are a few standard comeback lines:

•..*"Hey, why don't you have another drink and pass out!"*

•..*"I get paid to make an ass out of myself. What's your excuse?"*

•..*"I guess we serve anybody here!"*

•..*"I remember my first beer!"*

Intimidate them while remaining calm, bold and fearless, but not threatening. This is difficult to do, but crucial in handling a delicate and sometimes distressing situation. Above all, don't ever let it be visible that the heckler has succeeded in ruffling you.

Anyone who performs under a spotlight can become a possible target for verbal abuse and bodily harm. Alcohol - usually sold where you perform - affects people in different ways. Most people remain happy and pleasant, and some become even friendlier than usual. A few can become hostile and may even cause fights. Most performers who are not careful can become a target of such people and get themselves injured. If this happens to you, avoid all confrontations with such people, and do your best to ignore it as much as you can. Paying attention to such activity tends to encourage it; a beer bottle or even an ashtray can become a lethal weapon in the hands of a drunk. Have no part in it.

You may be confronted with jealous anger from someone's boyfriend/girlfriend or husband/wife. Some people are envious and have negative attitudes toward entertainers. Avoid, at all cost, the provoking of your clientele. Or, you may find that you have similar feelings when an audience member approaches your significant other in an annoying fashion. Be prepared to deal with these human problems in a diplomatic way.

NOTE: Please send any humorous "champ" comeback lines to Craig Colley c/o Houston Publishing. (The address is on the back cover) They will be reprinted as a service for musicians in future editions of this book.

CHAPTER SIXTEEN
CLIENTELE

You become established when you have a clientele - that is, a following of people who come to your performances. Your clientele will be as diverse as your music and shows. The type of clientele you develop will depend upon the type of club where you perform and how personable you are. Most nightclubs have a pre-set format that you will need to follow or fit into, and a major factor in any club's decision to hire you will be the type of clientele you have previously drawn.

Before and after performances, mingle with the crowd and make friends. It is easy to strike up a conversation because almost everyone will know who you are and usually will be interested in knowing more about you.

Obviously, playing older songs will bring in an older clientele; newer songs, the opposite. If you perform music from all different time periods, you will have a crossover of many age groups. From a business viewpoint, the older the crowd, the more money they will spend on drinking and tips; knowing this, you can market yourself and your music accordingly, but don't forget to play to all the members of the audience.

If you are unsure of what age bracket to gear yourself toward, check out other performers in the vicinity. See what's happening in different clubs. Acquire as much information as possible by listening to and talking with performers who are drawing the type of clientele in whom you are interested.

One of the most important and effective tools in dealing with your clientele is to remember the names of individuals after your first encounter with them. It makes them feel special and helps you to establish a good rapport with them. There are a few tricks you can use to accomplish this:

a) After introductions, memorize their name(s). Repeat them in your head over and over again. Do this at least five or six times, and then as soon as possible, call them by name several times when conversing.

b) Each person has his or her own personal characteristics. Utilize their most obvious one and associate it with their name.

c) Some people may always come with the same group, and usually out of that bunch, you will be able to remember one or two of their names. Then, at convenient times, you can ask what the other names are and eventually remember them all.

d) There are times when you will forget a good customer's name -which is very embarrassing. Listen to conversations (if they are near enough) and try to catch the person's name. Try not to let on when you can't remember who he or she is.

e) Review your guest book and mailing list cards. Remember a person's face for each name.

People like to be recognized.

Your friendship is a valuable asset in keeping a clientele, on or off stage.

CHAPTER SEVENTEEN
MAILING LISTS

Mailing lists are necessary for developing a clientele - a following of people who visit your shows frequently. Such lists can be tedious and costly, but if they are handled properly, they can be well worth the effort put into them.

Mailing lists may be developed through the use of guest books, table tents or address cards placed on tables. To remind people of their presence, mention from the stage, "If you are interested in being on my mailing list, please sign the guest book or fill out one of the cards that you see on your table with your name and address. I can then keep you informed of where I am performing."

A personal computer with software which enables you to generate mailing lists, along with a suitable printer, is the ideal way to keep your mailing list current. With a computer, you can add to your mailing list any new names that you get or, if you have a return address on your mailers, delete from it names and addresses of people who may have moved.

When mailing out information, use pre-stamped postcards (purchased from the Post Office in quantities), as they are cheaper than sending a letter and also save you the time of stamping each card. Investigate bulk mail rates. All information you wish to tell your followers about your performance engagements can be printed on the blank side of the postcard. Many times it is possible to work out a deal with a club where they pay for the postage of the mail cards and you provide the printing and labeling.

Your mailing list card is one place to use your eye-catching Logo. Even if people don't read what the card says, they will recognize your Logo which advertises you. To make it easy for your clientele to find you, print a small map showing the location of your gig, as well as the phone number.

CHAPTER EIGHTEEN

TRAVEL, TRANSPORTATION AND TAXES

Working in the music business can take you down the block or around the world. Your vehicle should be reliable and carry tools, such as a flashlight, flares, a small tool kit and a good spare tire. Know how to get to your destination and the amount of time it will take. Maps are always available. Join an emergency road service that covers you during a breakdown. Always have auto insurance (which is legally required in many states) and if affordable, a policy to cover the equipment that you are carrying in your vehicle. You might be in an accident, vandalized or burglarized.

Always carry a substantial amount of emergency cash, a major credit card and perhaps travelers checks when traveling on the road. Never let yourself be stranded away from home without any form of money.

When leaving any bar or nightclub, especially at closing time, drive defensively. In the event that you are pulled over, don't volunteer that you are an entertainer/musician; the police officer might assume you are under the influence of alcohol or drugs.

At tax time, you can deduct transportation costs if you keep receipts and an accurate account of your mileage. Keep good receipts of all your expenses, most of which will be deductible. Know the tax laws that affect you and acquire the services of an accountant who is knowledgeable in the music field.

CHAPTER NINETEEN
REWARDS AND FRINGE BENEFITS

Throughout time, musicians have possessed a unique ability derived from a God-given talent. It is a gift because, as in any other art form, either you "have it" or you don't. Levels and abilities of talents vary from one person to another, but it is how one applies it or puts it to work and grows musically that matters. It's an interesting and powerful experience to move an audience, to create a small fantasy where one can "get away from it all". Being on stage is being the center of attention. A career in the music industry is a constant struggle, but it has its rewards and fringe benefits that keep one going, including the self-satisfaction of making others feel happy, and applause and gratitude that comes naturally when you do so.

You will make friends and acquaintances, get cards and gifts, be invited to lunches, dinners and parties, and see new places and faces. The work hours are shorter than those of most other people, and your days are usually free.

As a professional entertainer, you are your own boss - and most important - you get paid for what you love to do - i.e.,

PLAY MUSIC!

CHAPTER TWENTY

SEASONS, HOLIDAY GIGS AND VACATIONS

Seasons

Holidays, three-day weekends and seasonal changes affect the marketplace. Weather is also a major factor in influencing people's moods and personalities (which surface when they go out for the evening). Usually, the better the weather, the larger the crowd. Generally, you can expect smaller than usual audiences on nights when there is heavy rain or snow outside.

As to specific seasons, spring and fall are inconsistent. You will have your share of good and bad nights. Winter is greatly influenced by the Christmas holiday season. It's likely that audiences will be large from Christmas through New Year's Eve, followed by a rather large letdown. January and February are quiet months. Summer, on the other hand, is the top season for the entertainment business. The weather is great and people are out and about enjoying it.

Holiday Gigs

Each year there are plenty of gigs that lead up to and fall upon each of the holidays. Be prepared in advance for those holidays that inspire their own styles of music. Christmas is an obvious example of this. Additionally, there is Saint Patrick's Day for Irish music, Fourth of July for patriotic songs, Labor Day for work/labor songs and school songs (since school starts up about that time), and Halloween which conjures up eerie, ghost-like or monster-type songs.

Because most holidays are incorporated into three-day weekends, it is difficult to predict the crowd. When a holiday falls on a Sunday or Monday, the previous weekend is often slow. On Thanksgiving Day, most places are closed unless they offer a turkey dinner special. Some areas have seasonal crowds or tourists because of their locations - e.g., ski resorts, summer camps and other vacation spots. Some locations operate all year long, but traffic varies (such as Fort Lauderdale, Florida or Palm Springs, California which are very popular with college students during Spring Break). The holidays of foreign countries often differ from ours, so it's advisable to check locally for this information. Gigs falling on days or nights after a big holiday (e.g., the day after Christmas or New Year's Day) will generally be slow.

Vacations

Vacations in the music business are all too often unplanned due to lack of work. If you are fortunate enough to be a steadily working musician, you will have the luxury of planning your time off. But when you leave, there will always be others waiting to take your job. Have a solid contract so that no problems arise when you return to or start your next gig. With good planning, you can schedule your vacations between engagements.

A good time to take off is the week prior to Christmas, unless you are doing private parties which normally pay better than most gigs. During this time, people spend most of their time with their families and do not go out to clubs as much. Generally, they also have less money because of what they've spent on gifts.

At times, the lifestyle of the working musician may seem exciting and glamorous. However, there are very few corporate-type benefits available to a musician. The reality is: If *you don't work, you don't get paid.* I don't know of any musician who has ever had a paid vacation (although I'm sure somebody, somewhere has).

There may be a conflict in your mind as to whether to keep working and making money, or to take a break. As much as you may love to play and perform, too much for too long can run you down and sometimes make you stale. Budget and plan for at least two weeks of vacation time a year.

If you are a traveling musician, it is sometimes possible to take short vacations between gigs when moving from town to town. Of course, one of the benefits of being a traveling musician is that your freedom during the daytime allows you to take in the sights of the locale in which you are working. Doing so is a great way to see the world, to grow and get paid at the same time. Working on a cruise ship is another possibility for combining working and vacationing - and it can be a great deal of fun.

There are many, many options to consider as you wind your way through the business and pleasure of making music - most of them intriguing. Be serious, careful and organized. Have a great time enjoying your life as you entertain, move people emotionally, and celebrate life with the music you play.

CHAPTER TWENTY-ONE

SONG DESCRIPTIONS

The next three chapters contain the most important information in this book. This chapter presents a list of categories which can be used in preparing a song set list. Chapters 22 & 23 provide a list of songs and an example on how to use this information. There is also a cut out page, *(a duplicate of this list on Page 87)*, at the back of the book for your convenience.

1. *Set openers*

2. *Songs to warm up your voice and crowd*

3. *Test songs for picking up tempo and energy in the room*

4. *Hand clapping:*

   A) *Tell audience to start clapping at beginning of song;*

   B) *Tell audience to start clapping in middle of song;*

   C) *Stop song in the middle to start clapping;*

   D) *Tell audience to clap with you and lead them at a break or drum fill in the song;*

   E) *Audience will usually start by themselves.*

5. *Singing along: Songs for the audience to sing along*

   A) *High or low singing parts in song for audience to sing;*

   B) *Male or female parts;*

   C) *Fill in the blank or singing "Heys";*

D) *All general singing, or tell audience it's their turn, and you stop singing, but continue playing;*

E) *Stop the song suddenly, and let audience continue by themselves for a moment;*

F) *Echo parts (You sing - They sing);*

G) *Divide audience into teams, possibly using some type of competition;*

H) *Counterpoint: Two-part singing at the same time.*

6. *Forceful and energetic:*

A) *When you've got the audience going or motivated;*

B) *Songs that work well in fast medleys.*

7. *Closing song*

8. *Encore song:*

A) *Has good start, but no finish; needs to go into another song.*

B) *Ending song in an encore medley.*

9. *Slow or dead spots: Times when your audience is not receptive, and it doesn't matter what you play (time killers)*

A) *Also very easy to sing*

10. *Heavily requested*

11. *Standard: Old or contemporary*

12. *Variety: Songs that are uniquely different from format*

13. *Love song dedications*

14. *Slow ballad or more songs with big, dramatic ending*

15. *Impression: Easy to do something that sounds like the artist*

16. *Joke or humorous songs*

   A) *R-Rated type*

17. *Trivia: Songs good for trivia questions or contests (represented by **"T"** in Chapter 22 - Song List By Category)*

18. *Request by certain artist*

19. *Medleys: Good for whole song or just part of it*

20. *Need the audience to really be listening so they can hear the words of the song in order for the song to go over. (Could apply to comedy or something serious.)*

21. *Set Ups: Songs that need or work well with an introduction*

   A) *Do you want to hear some more rock & roll?;*

   B) *Acting something out or telling a story before you begin the song;*

   C) *For certain groups of people in the audience:*

      i) *Vacationers;*

      ii) *People from other towns or countries;*

      iii) *People influenced by drugs;*

      iv) *Drinkers or drunks;*

      v) *Married or divorced;*

      vi) *Corrupt or degenerate;*

      vii) *Partyers;*

      viii) *Families (mother-daughter/father-son).*

   D) *Creating situations using male and female comparisons;*

   E) *Asking for finger snapping or hand clapping;*

F) *Utilizing any disturbance or occurrence at hand in the room;*

G) *Song by certain group or artist;*

H) *Do you feel like singing some more?;*

I) *Songs to whistle to.*

22. *Special Occasions:*

A) *Birthdays;*

B) *Anniversaries;*

C) *Hot date, wedding or honeymoon;*

D) *Full moon or weather phenomena;*

E) *Arriving or leaving town;*

F) *Meet someone or pick up night;*

G) *Holidays (Christmas, 4th of July, etc.);*

H) *Bar Room drinking or smoking song;*

I) *Employment: Hired or lost job;*

J) *Time of year (Seasons change, etc.);*

K) *Sad and lonely blues or break-up situation song.*

23. *City songs or songs from or about other countries*

24. *Songs from movies or musicals*

CHAPTER TWENTY-TWO

SONG LIST BY CATEGORY

This song list is designed to be used as a reference in devising a play or set list. Most of these songs are older, standard songs to know. However, they provide an overall view of what songs have lasting power and appeal to all ages of listeners. The songs have been categorized in alphabetical order under the following headings:

1) Slow ballads;

2) AC (Adult Contemporary) or MOR (Middle of the Road);

3) 50's;

4) 60's;

5) 70's, 80's and 90's;

6) C&W (Country and Western);

7) Blues;

8) Variety.

1. Slow Ballads

Against All Odds	T-1-2-9-18-22K-24
As Time Goes By	T-10-11-12-15
Auld Lang Syne	9-13-18
Bridge Over Troubled Water	1-10-11-18
Chariots of Fire	T-9-11-12-24
Colour My World	T-2-10-11-13-18
Could It Be Magic	10-11-14-18-19
Desperado	T-9-10-11-18
Feelings	10-11-13-16
Fire and Rain	T-2-9A-10-11-18
Heartlight	T-2-9-18-24
Hello	2-9-10-11-13-14-18-22BCF
Hello Again	13-18
I Just Called to Say I Love You	2-9-10-11-13-14-15-18-22BCF
I Write the Songs	2-9A-18
If	13-14-18
If You Could Read My Mind	T-2-9A-18
Imagine	T-9A-15-18
Lady	T-9-10-11-13-18

1. Slow Ballads, cont.

Lay Lady Lay	T-2-9A-18
Longer	2-9A-13-18
Love on the Rocks	2-9A-11-18-22H
Mandy	9-18
(This) Masquerade	T-9-18
Memory (Theme from "Cats")	1-2-10-11-14-24
Misty	9-10-11-12-13-15-18
Morning Has Broken	1-2-18
My Way	T-10-11-14-15-18
Open Arms	13-18
(The) Rose	9A-11-13
September Morn	1-2-9-10-11-13-14-18
Stuck On You	2-9-13-18-22BCF
Suddenly	1-2-9-13-22F
Time in a Bottle	T-2-9A-10-11-13-18-19
Truly	2-9-11-13-14-18-19-22BCF
(The) Way We Were	T-10-11-18
We're All Alone	9A-13-18
You Are the Sunshine of My Life	T-9-11-13-16-24
You Light Up My Life	10-11-13-16-24

2. AC (Adult Contemporary) or MOR (Middle of the Road) cont.

Against the Wind	T-9-18-19
Always a Woman	9-13-18
American Pie	T-2-3-5DE-11-14-18-19
Arthur's Theme	T-1-2-11-18-19-23-24
{Beginnings/Does Anybody Really Know What Time It Is?}	1-2-9-18-19
(On) Broadway	T-5EF-18-21-23
Cat in the Cradle	2-9A-18
City of New Orleans	1-2-9A-23
Country Roads	T-2-5-9-10-11-18-23
{Daniel/Tiny Dancer/Benny and the Jets}	T-1-2-3-9-10-18
Danny's Song	T-1-2-5E-9-13-18
Dock of the Bay	T-9-18-21C-23
Don't It Make My Brown Eyes Blue	2-9-10
Every Breath You Take	T-1-2-9-11-13-18
Everybody's Talkin' At Me	2-9A-22F-24
Father and Son	1-2-9A-18-21Cviii
For the Longest Time	1-2-3-5E-18-19-22CF
{Hotel California/Lyin' Eyes}	2-9-18-19
I Am I Said	2-9-18-19-23
It Might Be You	1-2-9-13-24
I've Got a Name	1-2-9A-18
Just the Way You Are	T-1-2-10-11-13-18-22B

2. AC (Adult Contemporary) or MOR (Middle of the Road) cont.

Kentucky Woman	1-2-9-18-19-23
Key Largo	1-2-9A-10-13-22K-23
Lawyers in Love	1-2-9-18
Leavin' on a Jet Plane	T-1-2-3-9A
Lookin' for Love	T-2-9A-11-22F-24
Margaritaville	T-1-2-3-9A-10-11-18-22H-23
Moondance	T-3-18-22D
Moonshadow	T-1-2-3-5E-9-18-19-22D
Mr. Bojangles	T-2-9-10-11
Nights in White Satin	2-9-12-18-19
Operator	2-9A-18-19
Peaceful Easy Feeling	T-1-2-9A-18-19
Piano Man	1-2-3-10-11-18
Raindrops	T-2-9-11-22E-24
Shame on the Moon	1-2-9A-18
{Solitary Man/Holly Holy/Song Sung Blue}	2-4E-5DE-9A-18-19
Steppin' Out	T-1-2-9-11-18-22F
Sunny	9-12-22D
Sweet Caroline	T-10-11-18-19
Take It Easy	T-18-19
You Are	1-2-9-13-18-22BCF
Your Song	T-1-2-9A-10-11-13-18

3. The 50's

Song	Code
Ain't That a Shame	T-5C-6AB-18-19
Blueberry Hill	T-5D-10-11-18-19
{Buddy Holly Medley: Oh Boy/Maybe Baby/Peggy Sue/That Will Be the Day}	3-4CDE-5DE-6A-10-11-18-22K
Bye Bye Love	T-4E-5DE-6A-10-11-18-22K
Chantilly Lace	T-3-4BE-5D-6A-10-11-12-18
{Devil in the Blue Dress/Good Golly Miss Molly/CC Ryder/Ginny Ginny/Long Tall Sally}	4ABCDE-5E-6A-7-8-10-11-18-21A
Diana	T-3-4E-5C-6AB-18-21H
Elvis Songs:	
All Shook Up	4E-5E-6A-10-11-15-18-19
Blue Suede Shoes	4E-5E-6A-7-8-10-11-15-18-21A
Can't Help Fallin' in Love With You	10-11-13-15-18
Heartbreak Hotel/Jailhouse Rock	4E-6A-7-8-10-11-15-18-21A
Hound Dog/Don't Be Cruel/Teddy Bear	4E-6A-11-15-18-21A
Return to Sender}	4E-5DE-6A-15-18-19
Framed	T-1-3-6A-12-21B-21C6
Great Balls of Fire	4E-5E-6A-7-8-11-15-18-19-21D-22C
Johnny B. Goode	4BE-5E-6A-7-8-10-11-18
Kansas City	4BCE-5BEF-6A-7-8-10-11-23
{La Bamba/Twist & Shout}	T-1-3-4AE-5DEH-6A-7-8-10-11-19-21A- 23
Little Darlin'	3-4E-5ADE-6A-7-8-11-16-19-21A
Love Potion No. 9	5C-6A-10-11-21C
Mabellene	T-3-4E-5D-6A-18-19

3. 50's, cont.

Mack the Knife	T-3-4E-5E-6A-10-11-18-21E
Old Time Rock & Roll	4CE-5DE-6A-7-8-10-11-18-21A
Pink Cadillac	T-3-4E-5D-6A-7-8-10-18-21A
Rock & Roll Music	3-6A-11-18-21A
Rock Around the Clock	T-4ABCE-5E-6A-10-11-18-21A
Rockin' Robin	T-4CE-5E-6A-19
Roll Over Beethoven	4D-6A-7-8-11
Runaround Sue	4E-5CD-6A-7-8-11-18-21B-22K
Runaway	T-5AE-6A-10-11-18-19
Sea of Love	T-1-2-9-9A-13-21Cv-22BC
(Whole Lot of) Shakin'	4BCE-5E-6-7-8-10-11-15-18-22C
Smoke Gets in Your Eyes	3-11-12-14-18-19-22H
{Splish Splash/At the Hop}	T-4E-5E-6A-11-18-21A
Stand By Me	T-1-2-3-4A-9-9A-10-11-12-22D
Summertime Blues	T-1-2-3-5E-6A-22J
Twist and Shout	4E-5EF-6A-7-8-11-21A-22C
Twistin' the Night Away	1-3-4BCE-5D-6A-18-19-21C-22AH
(The) Wanderer	T-5E-6A-18-22F
What'd I Say?	4ABE-5F-6A-10-11-15-18
Why Do Fools Fall in Love?	T-3-4E-9-18
{Wonderful World/Stay/Sherry/Breakin' Up is Hard to Do}	T-4BE-5E-6A-10-11-15-18

4. The 60's

{Beach Boys Medley: California Girls/Help Me Rhonda/Surfin' USA/Fun Fun Fun/Barbara Ann}	4ABE-5ABEG-6A-7-8-10-11-18-23
Born To Be Wild	T-5D-6A-7-8-11-18-19-21A-21Cvii-23
Brandy	T-2-9A-12-22H
Do Wa Diddy	4ACDE-5CF-6A-7-8-21AEH
Downtown	T-5C-6A-19-22F
Game of Love	T-3-5F-6A-12-19-22F
Gloria	T-5EF-8A-11-19
Happy Together	T-3-5EH-6A-10-11-18-19
{(There's a Kind of) Hush/Mrs. Brown, You've Got a Lovely Daughter/Henry the VIIIth}	T-3-4E-5CD-6B-10-11-12-18
I Feel Good	T-4E-5E-6A-7-8-18-19
I Think We're Alone Now	T-1-2-3-9-12-18
I'm a Believer	T-3-5E-19
Kind of a Drag	3-19
Light My Fire	T-9-14-18-19-21G
{Louie Louie/Hang on Sloopy}	T-5EF-6A-8A-10-11-19
{Mellow Yellow/Day Dream/	T-5E-6A-18-22F
Alice's Restaurant	T-3-5CD-21J
People Are Strange	T-2-3-12-18-19-21B
Pretty Woman	T-3-4BC-6A-11-18

4. The 60's, cont.

Proud Mary	T-1-5F-6A-11-18-19
Rainy Day Woman #12 and 35	5C-6A-15-18-19-21Cvi-22H-23
Satisfaction	4D-5E-6A-8A-10-11-15-18-22K
Secret Agent Man	T-2-5E-19
{Start Me Up/Jumpin' Jack Flash/	T-5C-6A-19-22F
Time Is On My Side}	1-5E-6A-8A-10-11-18
Under the Boardwalk	T-2-3-5EF-18-19
{Under My Thumb/Painted Black}	2-9-18-19
We Got To Get Out Of This Place	T-1-2-3-5E-6A-12-18-19-22E
Wild Thing	T-3-5D-12-19
Wooly Bully	5DE-19
Young Girl	T-5E-9-19
You've Really Got a Hold on Me	T-2-9-11-19
Beatle Songs:	
A Day in the Life	2-12-15-18-20-21Cii
A Hard Day's Night	5E-6A-8A-18-19-21B
All My Loving	2-3-9-18-19
Can't Buy Me Love	3-18-19
Do You Want to Know a Secret?	3-5EH-18-19
Eight Days a Week	3-4DE-5C-6A-18-19

4. The 60's, cont.

Get Back	T-1-2-3-9-18
Here, There and Everywhere	2-9-13-18-19
Hey, Jude	2-3-5DE-10-11-18-19
I Call Your Name	3-6A-18-19
I Saw Her Standing There	4E-5ACE-6A-7-8-11-18-19
I Should Have Known Better	4E-5AE-6A-18-19
I Will	2-13-18
In My Life	2-9-18-19
It's Only Love	3-9-18-19
Lady Madonna	4E-5C-6A-10-11-18-19
Let It Be	1-2-9-11-18
(The) Long and Winding Road	2-9-13-18
Michelle	2-9-18-19
No Reply	3-18-19
Ob-La-Di, Ob-La-Da	3-4E-5ADE-6A-18-19
Penny Lane	3-9-18-19-21Cii
Rocky Raccoon	2-3-9-18-19
Something	2-9-13-18-19
Yellow Submarine	3-4E-5DE
Yesterday	2-9-10-11-13-18-19

5. The 70's, 80's and 90's

After Midnight	T-1-3-4E-6A-9-18-21G
Allentown	T-1-2-3-18-23
At This Moment	T-9-13-14-18-24
Bad Bad Leroy Brown	1-3-4E-5CDE-6A-8-10-18-19-21H
Big Jim	1-2-3-4E-5DE-18-19
Country Roads	T-2-5E-9-18-23
Crazy Little Thing Called Love	1-2-6A-19
Devil Inside	T-1-2-3-9-12-18
End Of the Innocence	T-1-2-9-12-18
Every Time You Go	T-1-2-9A-12-13-18
Fire	T-1-2-3-5CDE-9-18
{Flashdance/Maniac}	1-2-3-24
Funeral for a Friend	1-2-9-10-14-18-19
I Guess That's Why they Call It the Blues	1-2-14-18
I Keep Forgettin'	2-9-18
If This Is It	1-3-6-18-19
I'm Still Standing	1-2-3-9-18-19
Joy To The World	T-1-2-3-4E-6A-7-8-10-19
Lady In Red	T-9-10-13-24
Logical Song	T-2-9-18
Lonely People	T-2-9-18-19-22K

5. The 70's, 80's and 90's, cont.

Maggie May	T-1-2-3-9-12-18
{Maneater/Kiss On My List}	1-3-18-19-22F
Norma Jean	1-2-9-10-18
One	T-3-9-19
Puttin' On the Ritz	3-4CE-5CE-10-11
Popsicle Toes	1-2-9A-12-18
Rebel Yell	T-5CDE-6A-7-8-18-21AGH-22C
Right Here Waitin' For You	T-1-2-9-12-13-18-22K
Rock This Town	1-3-4E-6A-7-8-10-11-18-19-21A
Roll With It	T-1-3-6A-9-18
Saturday Night	T-1-3-5EF-6A-7-8-18-21A
Some Kind of Friend	1-2-3-18
Stairway To Heaven	T-1-2-3-10-11-14-18
Still Rock & Roll To Me	3-6A-18-19
Suffragette City	T-1-3-5E-6A-7-8-18-19-22E
Tell Her About It	1-3-4E-18
Vincent (Starry, Starry Night)	2-9-18
Way It Is	T-1-2-4A-10-11-12-18
Wildfire	1-2-9A-18
You Are	1-3-9-13-18

6. C&W (Country & Western)

A Boy Named Sue	9-16-18-20
Act Naturally	T-3-4E-5C-6A
Duelin' Banjos	T-4ABCDE-6A-16-24
(The) Gambler	T-3-4CE-10-11-18
(The) Gay Caballero	16-20-21B
Hey, Good Lookin'	T-3-4E-5E-11-18
In the Kitchen	16-20-21F-22F
It's Hard to be Humble	T-3-4E-5E-16-20-21B
King of the Road	4BE-5CE-10-11-21H
Lookin' for Love	T-2-9A-11-22F-24
Lukenback, Texas (Basics of Love)	T-2-9A-18-23
Mama, Don't Let Your Babies Grow Up To Be Cowboys	T-3-10-11-18
Me & Bobby McGee	T-1-2-3-9-11-12-21Cii-21E
On the Road Again	T-3-4BE-10-11-18
Stick With the Dogs	16A-20-22F
Take This Job and Shove It	3-4E-5E-16-22J

7. Blues

Bring It On Home	12-16-20-22F
Georgia	2-9-10-11-15-18-23
Stormy Monday	9-11-12
Summertime Blues	9-10-11-12-18-22K

8. City Songs, Variety, or Show Tunes

Chicago	3-4E-5D-6-10-11-21Cii-23
Getting to Know You	T-24
Hava Nagila	3-4BE-5DE-6-11-21Cii
I Love L.A.	3-5CEF-6-7-10-23
(The) Lady Is a Tramp	1-2-9-11-12-18
MacNamera's Band	3-4ABCE-5D-6-11-21E-22GH-23
{My Favorite Things/Climb Every Mountain}	T-11-12-19-24
New York, New York	1-3-4BE-5CE-6-7-8-10-11-12-18-21C -23- 24
New York State of Mind	1-2-10-11-14-18-21
Oh, What a Beautiful Morning	5BCD-6A-11-12-24

CHAPTER TWENTY-THREE

SONG LIST BY DESCRIPTION

This chapter lists song suggestions in each category and in the same order as those listed in Chapter Twenty-one.

This is used the same way as the previous chapter except the songs are listed individually under each category. Because some songs can be used in several different ways, you will see some repetition under the following listings.

1. Set Openers

After Midnight
Against All Odds
Allentown
Arthur's Theme
Bad Bad Leroy Brown
{Beginnings/Does Anybody Really Know What time It Is?}
Big Jim
Bridge Over Troubled Water
City of New Orleans
Crazy Little Thing Called Love
{Daniel/Tiny Dancer/Benny and the Jets}
Danny's Song
Devil Inside
End of the Innocence
Every Breath You Take
Every Time You Go
Father and Son
Fire
{Flashdance/Maniac}

For the Longest Time
Framed
Funeral for a Friend
Get Back
I Guess That's Why They Call It the Blues
I Think We're Alone Now
If This Is It
I'm Still Standing
It Might Be You
I've Got A Name
Joy To the World
Just the Way You Are
Kentucky Woman
Key Largo
{La Bamba/Twist & Shout}
(The) Lady Is a Tramp
Lawyers in Love
Leavin' on a Jet Plane
Let It Be
Maggie May

1. Set Openers, cont.

Margaritaville
Me & Bobby McGee
Memories (Theme from "Cats")
Moonshadow
Morning Has Broken
New York, New York
New York State of Mind
Norma Jean
Peaceful Easy Feeling
Piano Man
Popsicle Toes
Proud Mary
Right Here Waitin' For You
Rock This Town
Roll With It
Saturday Night
Sea of Love

September Morn
Shame on the Moon
Some Kind of Friend
Stairway To Heaven
Stand By Me
{Start Me Up/Jumpin' Jack Flash/Time Is On My Side}
Steppin' Out
Suddenly
Suffragette City
Summertime Blues
Tell Her About It
Twistin' the Night Away
Way It Is
We Got To Get Out Of This Place
Wild Fire
You Are
Your Song

2. Warm up crowd and voice

A Day In the Life
A Hard Day's Night
Against All Odds
All My Loving
Allentown
American Pie
Arthur's Theme
{Beginnings/Does Anybody Really Know What Time It Is?}
Big Jim
Brandy
Cat In the Cradle
City of New Orleans
Color My World
Country Roads
Crazy Little Thing Called Love
{Daniel/Tiny Dancer/Benny and the Jets}
Danny's Song
Devil Inside
Don't It Make My Brown Eyes Blue
End Of the Innocence
Every Breath You Take

Every Time You Go
Everybody's Talkin' At Me
Father and Son
Fire
Fire and Rain
{Flashdance/Maniac}
For the Longest Time
Funeral For a Friend
Georgia
Get Back
Heartlight
Hello
Here, There and Everywhere
Hey, Jude
{Hotel California/Lyin' Eyes}
I Am I Said
I Guess That's Why They Call It the Blues
I Just Called To Say I Love You
I Keep Forgettin'
I Think We're Alone Now
I Will
I Write the Songs
If You Could Read My Mind

2. Warm up crowd and voice, cont.

I'm Still Standing
In My Life
It Might Be You
I've Got A Name
Joy To the World
Just the Way You Are
Kentucky Woman
Key Largo
(The) Lady Is a Tramp
Lawyers in Love
Lay Lady Lay
Leavin' on a Jet Plane
Let It Be
Logical Song
Lonely People
(The) Long and Winding Road
Longer
Lookin' For Love
Love On the Rocks
Lukenback, Texas (Basics of Love)
Maggie May
Margaritaville
Me & Bobby McGee
Memory (Theme from "Cats")
Michelle
Moonshadow
Morning Has Broken
Mr. Bojangles
New York State of Mind
Nights in White Satin
Norma Jean
Operator
Peaceful Easy Feeling

People Are Strange
Piano Man
Popsicle Toes
Raindrops
Right Here Waitin' For You
Rocky Raccoon
Sea of Love
Secret Agent Man
September Morn
Shame On the Moon
{Solitary Man/Holly Holy/Song Sung Blue}
Some Kind Of Friend
Something
Stairway To Heaven
Stand By Me
Steppin' Out
Stuck On You
Suddenly
Summertime Blues
Time In a Bottle
Truly
{Under My Thumb/Painted Black}
Under the Boardwalk
Vincent (Starry, Starry Night)
Way It Is
We Got To Get Out Of This Place
Wildfire
Yesterday
You Are
Your Song
You've Really Got a Hold On Me

3. Test songs for picking up tempo and energy in the room

Act Naturally
After Midnight
All My Loving
Allentown
American Pie
Bad Bad Leroy Brown
Big Jim
Can't Buy Me Love
Chantilly Lace

Chicago
{Daniel/Tiny Dancer/Benny and the Jets}
Devil Inside
Diana
Do You Want to Know a Secret?
Eight Days a Week
Fire
{Flashdance/Maniac}

3. Test songs for picking up tempo and energy in the room, cont.

For the Longest Time
Framed
(The) Gambler
Game of Love
Get Back
Happy Together
Have Nagila
Hey, Good Lookin'
Hey, Jude
{(There's a Kind of) Hush/Mrs. Brown,You've Got a Lovely Daughter/ Henry the VIIIth}
I Call Your Name
I Love L.A.
I Think We're Alone Now
If This Is It
I'm a Believer
I'm Still Standing
It's Hard to be Humble
It's Only Love
Joy To The World
Kind of a Drag
{La Bamba/Twist & Shout}
Leavin' On a Jet Plane
Little Darlin'
Mabellene
Mac the Knife
MacNamera's Band
Maggie May
Mama, Don't Let Your Babies Grow Up To Be Cowboys
{Maneater/Kiss On My List}
Margaritaville
Me & Bobby McGee
{Mellow Yellow/Day Dream/Alice's

Restaurant}
Moondance
Moonshadow
New York, New York
No Reply
Ob-La-Di, Ob-La-Da
On the Road Again
One
Penny Lane
People Are Strange
Piano Man
Pink Cadillac
Pretty Woman
Puttin' On the Ritz
Rock & Roll Music
Rock This Town
Rocky Raccoon
Roll With It
Saturday Night
Smoke Gets in Your Eyes
Some Kind of Friend
Stairway To Heaven
Stand By Me
Still Rock & Roll To Me
Suffragette City
Summertime Blues
Take This Job and Shove It
Tell Her About It
Twistin' the Night Away
Under the Boardwalk
We Got to Get Out of This Place
Why Do Fools Fall in Love?
Wild Thing
Yellow Submarine
You Are

4. Hand clapping:

A) Tell audience to start clapping at beginning of song;

B) Tell audience to start clapping in middle of song;

C) Stop song in the middle to start clapping;

D) Tell audience to clap with you and lead them at a break or drum fill in the song;

E) Audience will usually start by themselves.

Act Naturally [E]

After Midnight [E]

All Shook Up [E]

Bad Bad Leroy Brown [E]

{Beach Boys Medley: California Girls/ Help Me Rhonda/Surfin' USA/Fun Fun Fun/Barbara Ann} [ABE]

Big Jim [E]

Blue Suede Shoes [E]

{Buddy Holly Medley: Oh Boy/Maybe Baby/Peggy Sue/That Will Be the Day} [CDE]

Bye Bye Love [E]

Chantilly Lace [BE]

Chicago [E]

{Devil in the Blue Dress/Good Golly Miss Molly/CC Ryder/Ginny Ginny/ Long Tall Sally Medley} [ABCDE]

Diana [E]

Do Wa Diddy [ACDE]

Duelin' Banjos [ABCDE]

Eight Days a Week [DE]

(The) Gambler [CE]

Great Balls of Fire [E]

Hava nagila [BE]

Heartbreak Hotel/Jailhouse Rock/ Hound Dog/Don't Be Cruel/Teddy Bear} [E]

Hey, Good Lookin' [E]

{(There's a Kind of) Hush/Mrs. Brown, You've Got a Lovely Daughter/Henry the VIIIth} [E]

I Feel Good [E]

I Saw Her Standing There [E]

I Should Have Known Better[E]

It's Hard to be Humble [E]

Johnny B. Goode [BE]

Joy To The World [E]

Kansas City [BCE]

King of the Road BE]

{La Bamba/Twist & Shout} [AE]

Lady Madonna [E]

Little Darlin' [E]

Mabellene [E]

Mack the Knife [E]

MacNamera's Band [ABCE]

New York, New York [BE]

Ob-La-Di, Ob-La-Da [E]

Old Time Rock & Roll [CE]

On the Road Again [BE]

Pink Cadillac [E]

Pretty Woman [BC]

Puttin' On the Ritz [CE]

Return to Sender [E]

Rock Around the Clock [ABCE]

Rock This Town [E]

Rockin' Robin [CE]

Roll Over Beethoven [D]

Runaround Sue [E]

Satisfaction [D]

(Whole Lot of) Shakin' [BCE]

{Solitary Man/Holly Holy/Song Sung Blue} [E]

{Splish Splash/At the Hop} [E]

Stand By Me [A]

Take This Job and Shove It [E]

Tell Her About It [E]

Twistin' the Night Away [BCE]

4. Hand clapping, cont.

Way It Is **[A]**
What'd I Say? **[ABE]**
Why Do Fools Fall in Love? **[E]**
{Wonderful World/Stay/Sherry/
Breakin' Up is Hard to Do} **[BE]**
Yellow Submarine **[E]**

5. Singing along:

A) High or low singing parts in song for audience to sing;

B) Male or female parts;

C) Fill in the blank or singing "Heys";

D) All general singing, or tell audience it's their turn, and you stop singing, but continue playing;

E) Stop the song suddenly, and let audience continue by themselves for a moment;

F) Echo parts (You sing - They sing);

G) Divide audience into teams, possibly using some type of competition;

H) Counterpoint: Two-part singing at the same time.

A Hard Day's Night **[E]**
Act Naturally **[C]**
Ain't That a Shame **[C]**
All Shook Up **[E]**
American Pie **[DE]**
Bad Bad Leroy Brown **[CDE]**
{Beach Boys Medley: California Girls/
Help Me Rhonda/Surfin' USA/Fun Fun
Fun/Barbara Ann} **[ABEG]**
Big Jim **[DE]**
Blue Suede Shoes **[E]**
Blueberry Hill **[D]**
Born To Be Wild **[D]**
(On) Broadway **[EF]**
{Buddy Holly Medley: Oh Boy/Maybe

Baby/Peggy Sue/That Will Be the Day}
[DE]
Bye Bye Love **[DE]**
Chantilly Lace **[D]**
Chicago **[D]**
Country Roads **[E]**
Danny's Song **[E]**
{Devil in the Blue Dress/Good Golly
Miss Molly/CC Ryder/Ginny Ginny/
Long Tall Sally Medley} **E]**
Diana **[C]**
Do Wa Diddy **[CF]**
Do You Want to Know a Secret? **[EH]**
Downtown **[C]**
Eight Days a Week **[C]**

4

5. Singing along, cont.

Fire [CDE]
For the Longest Time [E]
Game of Love [F]
Gloria [EF]
Great Balls of Fire [E]
Happy Together [EH]
Hava nagila [DE]
Hey, Good Lookin' [E]
Hey, Jude [DE]
{(There's a Kind of) Hush/Mrs. Brown,
You've Got a Lovely Daughter/Henry
the VIIIth} [CD]
I Feel Good [E]
I Love L.A. [CEF]
I Saw Her Standing There [ACE]
I Should Have Known Better [AE]
I'm a Believer [E]
It's Hard to be Humble [E]
Johnny B. Goode [E]
Kansas City
King of the Road [CE]
{La Bamba/Twist & Shout} [DEH]
Lady Madonna
Little Darlin'   [ADE]
{Louie Louie/Hang on Sloopy} [EF]
Love Potion No. 9
Mabellene [D]
Mack the Knife [E]
MacNamera's Band [D]
{Mellow Yellow/Day Dream/Alice's
Restaurant} [CD]
Moonshadow [E]
New York, New York [CE]
Ob-La-Di, Ob-La-Da [ADE]
Oh, What a Beautiful Morning

Old Time Rock & Roll [DE]
Pink Cadillac [D]
Proud Mary [F]
Puttin' On the Ritz [CE]
Rainy Day Woman #12 and 35 [C]
Rebel Yell [CDE]
Return to Sender [DE]
Rock Around the Clock [E]
Rockin' Robin [E]
Runaround Sue [AE]
Runaway [AE]
Satisfaction [E]
Saturday Night [EF]
Secret Agent Man [E]
(Whole Lot of) Shakin' [E]
{Solitary Man/Holly Holy/Song Sung
Blue} [DE]
{Splish Splash/At the Hop} [E]
{Start Me Up/Jumpin' Jack Flash/Time
Is On My Side} [E]
Suffragette City [E]
Summertime Blues [E]
Take This Job and Shove It [E]
Twist and Shout [EF]
Twistin' the Night Away [D]
Under the Boardwalk [EF]
(The) Wanderer [E]
We Got to Get Out of This Place [E]
What'd I Say? [F]
Wild Thing [D]
{Wonderful World/Stay/Sherry/
Breakin' Up is Hard to Do} [E]
Wooly Bully [DE]
Yellow Submarine [DE]
Young Girl

6. Forceful and energetic: (all songs 6A except those with [B]).

A) When you've got the audience going or motivated;

B) Songs that work well in fast medleys.

A Hard Day's Night
Act Naturally
After Midnight
Ain't That a Shame **[B]**
All Shook Up
Bad Bad Leroy Brown
{Beach Boys Medley: California Girls/
Help Me Rhonda/Surfin' USA/Fun Fun
Fun/Barbara Ann}
Blue Suede Shoes
Born To Be Wild
{Buddy Holly Medley: Oh Boy/Maybe
Baby/Peggy Sue/That Will Be the Day}
Bye Bye Love
Chantilly Lace
Chicago
Crazy Little Thing Called Love
{Devil in the Blue Dress/Good Golly
Miss Molly/CC Ryder/Ginny Ginny/
Long Tall Sally Medley}
Diana **[B]**
Do Wa Diddy
Downtown
Duelin' Banjos
Eight Days a Week
Framed
Game of Love
Great Balls of Fire
Happy Together
Have Nagila
{Heartbreak Hotel/Jailhouse Rock/
Hound Dog/Don't Be Cruel/Teddy
Bear}
{(There's a Kind of) Hush/Mrs. Brown,
You've Got a Lovely Daughter/Henry
the VIIIth} **[B]**
I Call Your Name -I Feel Good
I Love L.A.
I Saw Her Standing There -I Should
Have Known Better
If This Is It
Johnny B. Goode
Joy to the World

Kansas City
{La Bamba/Twist & Shout}
Lady Madonna
Little Darlin'- {Louie Louie/Hang on
Sloopy}
Love Potion No. 9
Mabellene
Mac the Knife
MacNamera's Band
New York, New York
Ob-La-Di, Ob-La-Da
Oh, What a Beautiful Morning
Old Time Rock & Roll
Pink Cadillac
Pretty Woman
Proud Mary
Rainy Day Woman #12 and 35
Rebel Yell
Return to Sender
Rock & Roll Music
Rock Around the Clock
Rock This Town
Rockin' Robin
Roll Over Beethoven
Roll With It
Runaround Sue
Runaway
Satisfaction
Saturday Night
(Whole Lot of) Shakin'
Splish Splash/At the Hop
{Start Me Up/Jumpin' Jack Flash/Time
Is On My Side}
Still Rock & Roll To Me
Suffragette City
Summertime Blue
Twist and Shout
Twistin' the Night Away
(The) Wanderer
We Got to Get Out of This Place
What'd I Say?
{Wonderful World/Stay/Sherry/
Breakin' Up is Hard to Do}

7. Closing song:

{Beach Boys Medley: California Girls/
Help Me Rhonda/Surfin' USA/Fun Fun
Fun/Barbara Ann}
Blue Suede Shoes
Born To Be Wild
{Devil in the Blue Dress/Good Golly
Miss Molly/CC Ryder/Ginny Ginny/
Long Tall Sally Medley}
Do Wa Diddy
Great Balls of Fire
{Heartbreak Hotel/Jailhouse Rock}
I Feel Good
I Love L.A.
I Saw Her Standing There
Johnny B. Goode
Joy to the World

Kansas City
{La Bamba/Twist & Shout}
Little Darlin'
New York, New York
Old Time Rock & Roll
Pink Cadillac
Rebel Yell
Rock This Town
Roll Over Beethoven
Runaround Sue
Saturday Night
(Whole Lot of) Shakin'
Still Rock
& Roll To Me
Suffragette City
Twist and Shout

8. Encore song:

A) Has good start, but no finish; needs to go into another song.

B) Ending song in an encore medley.

A Hard Day's Night [A]
Bad Bad Leroy Brown [B]
{Beach Boys Medley: California Girls/
Help Me Rhonda/Surfin' USA/Fun Fun
Fun/Barbara Ann} [B]
Blue Suede Shoes [B]
Born To Be Wild [B]
{Devil in the Blue Dress/Good Golly
Miss Molly/CC Ryder/Ginny Ginny/
Long Tall Sally Medley}
Do Wa Diddy
Gloria [A]
Great Balls of Fire
{Heartbreak Hotel/Jailhouse Rock}
I Feel Good
I Saw Her Standing There
Johnny B. Goode

Joy to the World
Kansas City
{La Bamba/Twist & Shout}
Little Darlin'
{Louie Louie/Hang on Sloopy} [A]
New York, New York
Old Time Rock & Roll
Pink Cadillac
Rebel Yell
Rock This Town
Roll Over Beethoven
Runaround Sue
Satisfaction [A]
Saturday Night
(Whole Lot of) Shakin'
Suffragette City
Twist and Shout

9. Slow or dead spots: Times when your audience is not receptive, and it doesn't matter what you play (time killers)

A) Also very easy to sing

A Boy Named Sue
After Midnight
Against All Odds
Against the Wind
All My Loving
Always a Woman
At This Moment
Auld Lang Syne
{Beginnings/Does Anybody Really Know What Time It Is?}
Brandy
Cat in the Cradle **[A]**
Chariots of Fire
City of New Orleans **[A]**
Country Roads
{Daniel/Tiny Dancer/Benny and the Jets}
Danny's Song
Desperado
Devil Inside
Dock of the Bay
Don't It Make My Brown Eyes Blue
End Of the Innocence
Every Breath You Take
Every Time You Go **[A]**
Everybody's Talkin' At Me **[A]**
Father and Son **[A]**
Fire and Rain **[A]**
Funeral for a Friend
Georgia
Get Back
Heartlight
Hello
Here, There and Everywhere
{Hotel California/Lyin' Eyes}
I Am I Said
I Just Called to Say I Love You
I Keep Forgettin'
I Think We're Alone Now
If You Could Read My Mind **[A]**
I'm Still Standing

Imagine **[A]**
In My Life
It Might Be You
It's Only Love
I've Got a Name **[A]**
I Write the Songs **[A]**
Kentucky Woman
Key Largo **[A]**
Lady
Lady In Red
(The) Lady Is a Tramp
Lawyers in Love
Lay Lady Lay **[A]**
Leavin' on a Jet Plane
Let It Be
Light My Fire
Logical Song
Lonely People
(The) Long and Winding Road
Longer **[A]**
Lookin' for Love **[A]**
Love on the Rocks **[A]**
Lukenback, Texas (Basics of Love) **[A]**
Maggie May
Mandy
Margaritaville **[A]**
(This) Masquerade
Me & Bobby McGee
Michelle
Misty
Moonshadow
Mr. Bojangles
Nights in White Satin
Norma Jean
One
Operator **[A]**
Peaceful Easy Feeling **[A]**
Penny Lane
Popsicle Toes **[A]**
Raindrops
Right Here Waitin' For You

9. Slow or dead spots, cont.

Rocky Raccoon
Roll With It
(The) Rose [A]
Sea of Love [A]
September Morn
Shame on the Moon [A]
(Solitary Man/Holly Holy/Song Sung
Blue) [A]
Something
Stand By Me [A]
Steppin' Out
Stormy Monday
Stuck On You
Suddenly
Summertime Blues

Sunny
Time in a Bottle [A]
Truly
{Under My Thumb/Painted Black}
Vincent (Starry, Starry Night)
We're All Alone [A]
Why Do Fools Fall in Love?
Wildfire [A]
Yesterday
You Are
You Are the Sunshine of My Life
Young Girl
Your Song [A]
You've Really Got a Hold on Me

10. Heavily requested

All Shook Up
As Time Goes By
Bad Bad Leroy Brown
{Beach Boys Medley: California Girls/
Help Me Rhonda/Surfin' USA/Fun Fun
Fun/Barbara Ann}
Blue Suede Shoes
Blueberry Hill
Bridge Over Troubled Water
{Buddy Holly Medley: Oh Boy/Maybe
Baby/Peggy Sue/That Will Be the Day}
Bye Bye Love
Can't Help Fallin' in Love With You
Chantilly Lace
Chicago
Color My World
Could It Be Magic
Country Roads
Daniel/Tiny Dancer/Benny and the
Jets
Desperado
{Devil in the Blue Dress/Good Golly
Miss Molly/CC Ryder/Ginny Ginny/
Long Tall Sally Medley}
Don't It Make My Brown Eyes Blue
Feelings

Fire and Rain
Funeral for a Friend
(The) Gambler
Georgia
Happy Together
{Heartbreak Hotel/Jailhouse Rock}
Hello
Hey, Jude
{(There's a Kind of) Hush/Mrs. Brown,
You've Got a Lovely Daughter/Henry
the VIIIth}
I Just Called to Say I Love You
I Love L.A.
Johnny B. Goode
Joy to the World
Just the Way You Are
Kansas City
Key Largo
King of the Road
{La Bamba/Twist & Shout}
Lady
Lady in Red
Lady Madonna
{Louie Louie/Hang on Sloopy}
Love Potion No. 9
Mack the Knife

10. Heavily requested, cont.

Mama, Don't Let Your Babies Grow Up
To Be Cowboys
Margaritaville
Memories (Theme from "Cats")
Misty
Mr. Bojangles
My Way
New York, New York
New York State of Mind
Norma Jean
Old Time Rock & Roll
On the Road Again
Piano Man
Pink Cadillac
Puttin' On the Ritz
Rock Around the Clock
Rock This Town
Runaway

Satisfaction
September Morn
(Whole Lot of) Shakin'
Stairway to Heaven
Stand By Me
{Start Me Up/Jumpin' Jack Flash/Time Is On My Side}
Summertime Blues
Sweet Caroline
Time in a Bottle
Way It Is
(The) Way We Were
What'd I Say?
{Wonderful World/Stay/Sherry/Breakin' Up is Hard to Do}
Yesterday
You Light Up My Life
Your Song

11. Standard: Old or Contemporary

All Shook Up
American Pie
Arthur's Theme
As Time Goes By
{Beach Boys Medley: California Girls/Help Me Rhonda/Surfin' USA/Fun Fun Fun/Barbara Ann}
Blue Suede Shoes
Blueberry Hill
Born To Be Wild
Bridge Over Troubled Water
{Buddy Holly Medley: Oh Boy/Maybe Baby/Peggy Sue/That Will Be the Day}
Bye Bye Love
Can't Help Fallin' in Love With You
Chantilly Lace
Chariots of Fire
Chicago
Color My World
Could It Be Magic
Country Roads
Desperado
{Devil in the Blue Dress/Good Golly Miss Molly/ CCRyder/Ginny Ginny/

Long Tall Sally Medley}
Every Breath You Take
Feelings
Fire and Rain
(The) Gambler
Georgia
Gloria
Great Balls of Fire
Happy Together
Have Nagila
{Heartbreak Hotel/Jailhouse Rock}
Hello
Hey, Good Lookin'
Hey, Jude
{Hound Dog/Don't Be Cruel/Teddy Bear}
{(There's a Kind of) Hush/Mrs. Brown, You've Got a Lovely Daughter/Henry the VIIIth}
I Just Called To Say I Love You
I Saw Her Standing There
Johnny B. Goode
Just the Way You Are
Kansas City
King of the Road

11. Standard: Old or Contemporary, cont.

{La Bamba/Twist & Shout}
Lady
(The) Lady Is a Tramp
Lady Madonna
Let It Be
Little Darlin'
Lookin' For Love -{Louie Louie/Hang on Sloopy}
Love on the Rocks
Love Potion No. 9
Mack the Knife
MacNamera's Band
Mama, Don't Let Your Babies Grow Up To Be Cowboys
Margaritaville
Me & Bobby McGee
Memory (Theme from "Cats")
Misty
Mr. Bojangles
{My Favorite Things/Climb Every Mountain}
My Way
New York, New York
New York State of Mind
Oh, What a Beautiful Morning
Old Time Rock & Roll
On the Road Again
Piano Man
Pretty Woman
Proud Mary
Puttin' On the Ritz
Raindrop
Rock & Roll Music

Rock Around the Clock
Rock This Town
Roll Over Beethoven
(The) Rose
Runaround Sue
Runaway
Satisfaction
September Morn
(Whole Lot of) Shakin'
Smoke Gets in Your Eyes
{Splish Splash/At the Hop}
Stairway To Heaven
Stand By Me
{Start Me Up/Jumpin' Jack Flash/Time Is On My Side}
Steppin' Out
Stormy Monday
Summertime Blues
Sweet Caroline
Time in a Bottle
Truly
Twist and Shout
Way It Is
(The) Way We Were
What'd I Say?
{Wonderful World/Stay/Sherry/Breakin' Up is Hard to Do}
Yesterday
You Are the Sunshine of My Life
You Light Up My Life
Your Song
You've Really Got a Hold on Me

12. Variety: Songs that are uniquely different from format

A Day in the Life
As Time Goes By
Brandy
Bring It On Home
Chantilly Lace
Chariots of Fire
Devil Inside
End of the Innocence

Every Time You Go
Game of Love
{(There's a Kind of) Hush/Mrs. Brown,You've Got a Lovely Daughter/Henry the VIIIth}
I Think We're Alone Now
(The) Lady Is a Tramp
Maggie May

12. Variety, cont.

Me & Bobby McGee
Misty
{My Favorite Things/Climb Every Mountain}
New York, New York
Nights in White Satin
Oh, What a Beautiful Morning
People Are Strange
Popsicle Toes

Right Here Waitin' for You
Smoke Gets in Your Eyes
Stand By Me
Stormy Monday
Summertime Blues
Sunny
Way It Is
We Got to Get Out of This Place
Wild Thing

13. Love song dedications

Always a Woman
At This Moment
Auld Lang Syne
Can't Help Fallin' In Love With You
Color My World
Danny's Song
Every Breath You Take
Every Time You Go
Feelings
Hello
Hello Again
Here, There and Everywhere
I Just Called to Say I Love You
I Will
If
It Might Be You
Just the Way You Are
Key Largo
Lady
Lady in Red

(The) Long and Winding Road
Longer
Misty
Open Arms
Right Here Waitin' For You
(The) Rose
Sea of Love
September Morn
Something
Stuck On You
Suddenly
Time in a Bottle
Truly
We're All Alone
Yesterday
You Are
You Are the Sunshine of My Life
You Light Up My Life
Your Song

14. Slow ballad or more songs with big, dramatic ending

American Pie
At This Moment
Could It Be Magic
Funeral for a Friend
Hello
I Guess That's Why They Call It the Blues
I Just Called to Say I Love You

If
Light My Fire
Memories (Theme from "Cats")
My Way
New York State of Mind
September Morn
Smoke Gets In Your Eyes
Stairway to Heaven
Truly

15. Impression: Easy to do something that sounds like the artist

A Day in the Life
All Shook Up
As Time Goes By
Blue Suede Shoes
Can't Help Fallin' in Love With You
{Devil in the Blue Dress/Good Golly Miss Molly/CC Ryder/Ginny Ginny/Long Tall Sally Medley}
Georgia
Great Balls of Fire
{Heartbreak Hotel/Jailhouse Rock/Hound Dog/Don't Be Cruel/Teddy Bear}

I Just Called to Say I Love You
Imagine
Misty
My Way
Rainy Day Woman #12 and 35
Return to Sender
Satisfaction
(Whole Lot of) Shakin'
What'd I Say?
{Wonderful World/Stay/Sherry/Breakin' Up is Hard to Do}

16. Joke or Humorous Songs

A) R-Rated type

A Boy Named Sue
Bring It On Home
Duelin' Banjos
Feelings
(The) Gay Caballero [A]

It's Hard to be Humble
Little Darlin'
Stick With the Dogs [A]
Take This Job and Shove It
You Are the Sunshine of My Life
You Light Up My Life

17. (T) Trivia: Songs good for trivia questions or contests
(represented by "T" in Chapter 22 - Song List By Category)

Act Naturally
After Midnight
Against All Odds
Against the Wind
Ain't That a Shame
Allentown
American Pie
Arthur's Theme
As Time Goes By
At This Moment
Blueberry Hill
Born To Be Wild
Brandy
(On) Broadway

Bye Bye Love
Chantilly Lace
Chariots of Fire
Color My World
Country Roads
{Daniel/Tiny Dancer/Benny and the Jets}
Danny's Song
Desperado
Devil Inside
Diana
Dock of the Bay
Downtown
Duelin' Banjos

17. (T) Trivia, cont.

End Of the Innocence
Every Breath You Take
Every Time You Go
Fire
Fire and Rain
Framed
(The) Gambler
Game of Love
Get Back
Getting to Know You
Gloria
Happy Together
Heartlight
Hey, Good Lookin'
{(There's a Kind of) Hush/Mrs. Brown, You've Got a Lovely Daughter/Henry the VIIIth}
I Feel Good
I Think We're Alone Now
If You Could Read My Mind
I'm a Believer
Imagine
It's Hard to be Humble
Joy To The World
Just the Way You Are
{La Bamba/Twist & Shout}
Lady
Lady In Red
Lay Lady Lay
Leavin' on a Jet Plane
Light My Fire
Logical Song
Lonely People
Lookin' for Love
{Louie Louie/Hang on Sloopy}
Lukenback, Texas (Basics of Love)
Mabellene
Mac the Knife
Maggie May
Mama, Don't Let Your Babies Grow Up To Be Cowboys
Margaritaville
(This) Masquerade
Me & Bobby McGee
{Mellow Yellow/Day Dream/Alice's Restaurant}

Moondance
Moonshadow
Mr. Bojangles
{My Favorite Things/Climb Every Mountain}
My Way
On the Road Again
One
Peaceful Easy Feeling
People Are Strange
Pink Cadillac
Pretty Woman
Proud Mary
Raindrops
Rebel Yell
Right Here Waitin' For You
Rock Around the Clock
Rockin' Robin
Roll With It
Runaway
Saturday Night
Sea of Love
Secret Agent Man
{Splish Splash/At the Hop}
Stairway To Heaven
Stand By Me
Steppin' Out
Suffragette City
Summertime Blues
Sweet Caroline
Take It Easy
Time in a Bottle
Under the Boardwalk
(The) Wanderer
Way It Is
(The) Way We Were
We Got to Get Out of This Place
Why Do Fools Fall in Love?
Wild Thing
{Wonderful World/Stay/Sherry/Breakin' Up is Hard to Do}
You Are the Sunshine of My Life
Young Girl
Your Song
You've Really Got a Hold on Me

18. Request by certain artist

A Boy Named Sue
A Day in the Life
A Hard Day's Night
After Midnight
Ain't That a Shame
Against All Odds
Against the Wind
All My Loving
All Shook Up
Allentown
Always a Woman
American Pie
Arthur's Theme
At This Moment
Auld Lang Syne
Bad Bad Leroy Brown
{Beach Boys Medley: California Girls/
Help Me Rhonda/Surfin' USA/Fun Fun
Fun/Barbara Ann}
{Beginnings/Does Anybody Really
Know What Time It Is?}
Big Jim
Blue Suede Shoes
Blueberry Hill
Born To Be Wild
Bridge Over Troubled Water
(On) Broadway
{Buddy Holly Medley: Oh Boy/Maybe
Baby/Peggy Sue/That Will Be the Day}
Bye Bye Love
Can't Buy Me Love
Can't Help Fallin' In Love
Cat in the Cradle
Chantilly Lace
Color My World
Could It Be Magic
Country Roads
{Daniel/Tiny Dancer/Benny and the
Jets}
Danny's Song
Desperado
{Devil in the Blue Dress/Good Golly
Miss Molly/CC Ryder/Ginny Ginny/
Long Tall Sally Medley}
Devil Inside
Diana

Do You Want to Know a Secret?
Dock of the Bay
Eight Days a Week
End Of the Innocence
Every Breath You Take
Every Time You Go
Father and Son
Fire
Fire and Rain
For the Longest Time
Funeral for a Friend
(The) Gambler
Georgia
Get Back
Great Balls of Fire
Happy Together
{Heartbreak Hotel/Jailhouse Rock}
Heartlight
Hello
Hello Again
Here, There and Everywhere
Hey, Good Lookin'
Hey, Jude
{Hotel California/Lyin' Eyes} -{Hound
Dog/Don't Be Cruel/Teddy Bear}
{(There's a Kind of) Hush/Mrs. Brown,
You've Got a Lovely Daughter/Henry
the VIIIth}
I Am I Said
I Call Your Name
I Feel Good
I Guess That's Why they Call It the
Blues
I Just Called to Say I Love You
I Keep Forgettin'
I Saw Her Standing There
I Should Have Known Better
I Think We're Alone Now
I Will
I Write the Songs
If
If This Is It
If You Could Read My Mind
I'm Still Standing
Imagine
In My Life

18. Request by certain artist, cont.

It's Only Love
I've Got a Name
Johnny B. Goode
Just the Way You Are
Kentucky Woman
Lady
(The) Lady Is a Tramp
Lady Madonna
Lawyers in Love
Lay Lady Lay
Let It Be
Light My Fire
Logical Song
Lonely People
(The) Long and Winding Road
Longer
Love on the Rocks
Lukenback, Texas (Basics of Love)
Mabellene
Mac the Knife
MacNamera's Band
Maggie May
Mama, Don't Let Your Babies Grow Up
To Be Cowboys
Mandy
Maneater/Kiss On My List
Margaritaville
(This) Masquerade
Michelle
Misty
Moondance
Moonshadow
Morning Has Broken
My Way
New York, New York
New York State of Mind
Nights in White Satin
No Reply
Norma Jean
Ob-La-Di, Ob-La-Da
Old Time Rock & Roll
On the Road Again
Open Arms
Operator
Peaceful Easy Feeling
Penny Lane

People Are Strange
Piano Man
Pink Cadillac
Popsicle Toes
Pretty Woman
Proud Mary
Rainy Day Woman #12 and 35
Rebel Yell
Return to Sender
Right Here Waitin' For You
Rock & Roll Music
Rock Around the Clock
Rock This Town
Rocky Raccoon
Roll With It
Runaround Sue
Runaway
Satisfaction
Saturday Night
September Morn
(Whole Lot of) Shakin'
Shame on the Moon
Smoke Gets in Your Eyes
{Solitary Man/Holly Holy/Song Sung Blue}
Some Kind of Friend
Something
Splish Splash/At the Hop
Stairway To Heaven
{Start Me Up/Jumpin' Jack Flash/Time Is On My Side}
Steppin' Out
Still Rock & Roll To Me
Stuck on You
Suffragette City
Summertime Blues
Sweet Caroline
Take It Easy
Tell Her About It
Time in a Bottle
Truly
Twistin' the Night Away
Under the Boardwalk
{Under My Thumb/Painted Black}
Vincent (Starry, Starry Night)
(The) Wanderer

18. Request by certain artist, cont.

Way It Is
The) Way We Were
We Got to Get Out of This Place
We're All Alone
What'd I Say?
Why Do Fools Fall in Love?

Wildfire
{Wonderful World/Stay/Sherry/
Breakin' Up is Hard to Do}
Yesterday
You Are
Your Song

19. Medleys: Good for whole song or just part of it

A Hard Day's Night
Against the Wind
Ain't That a Shame
All My Loving
All Shook Up
American Pie
Arthur's Theme
Bad Bad Leroy Brown
Big Jim
{Beginnings/Does Anybody Really
Know What Time It Is?}
Blueberry Hill
Born To Be Wild
Can't Buy Me Love
Could It Be Magic
Crazy Little Thing Called Love
Do You Want to Know a Secret? -
Downtown
Eight Days a Week
For the Longest Time
Funeral for a Friend
Game of Love
Gloria
Great Balls of Fire
Happy Together
Here, There and Everywhere
Hey, Jude
{Hotel California/Lyin' Eyes}
I Am I Said
I Call Your Name
I Feel Good
I Saw Her Standing There
I Should Have Known Better
If This Is It
I'm a Believer
I'm Still Standing
In My Life

It's Only Love
Joy To The World
Kentucky Woman
Kind of a Drag
{La Bamba/Twist & Shout}
Lady Madonna
Light My Fire
Little Darlin'
Lonely People
(The) Long and Winding Road
{Louie Louie/Hang on Sloopy}
Mabellene
{Maneater/Kiss On My List}
Michelle
Moonshadow
{My Favorite Things/Climb Every
Mountain}
Nights in White Satin
No Reply
Ob-La-Di, Ob-La-Da
One
Operator
Peaceful Easy Feeling
Penny Lane
People Are Strange
Proud Mary
Rainy Day Woman #12 and 35
Return to Sender
Rock This Town
Rockin' Robin
Rocky Raccoon
Runaway
Secret Agent Man
Smoke Gets In Your Eyes
{Solitary Man/Holly Holy/Song Sung
Blue}
Something

19. Medleys: Good for whole song or just part of it, cont.

Still Rock & Roll To Me
Suffragette City
Sweet Caroline
Take It Easy
Time in a Bottle
Truly
Twistin' The Night Away
Under My Thumb

Under the Boardwalk
We Got to Get Out of This Place
Wild Thing
Wooly Bully
Yesterday
Young Girl
You've Really Got a Hold on Me

20. Need the audience to really be listening so they can hear the words of the song in order for the song to go over. (Could apply to comedy or something serious.)

A Boy Named Sue
A Day in the Life
Bring It On Home
(The) Gay Caballero

In the Kitchen
It's Hard to be Humble
Stick With the Dogs

21. Set Ups: Songs that need or work well with an introduction:

A) Do you want to hear some more rock & roll?;

B) Acting something out or telling a story before you begin the song;

C) For certain groups of people in the audience:

    i)   Vacationers;

    ii)   People from other towns or countries;

    iii)   People influenced by drugs;

    iv)   Drinkers or drunks;

    v)   Married or divorced;

    vi)   Corrupt or degenerate;

    vii)   Partyers;

    viii)   Families (mother-daughter/father-son).

21. Set Ups, cont.

D) Creating situations using male and female comparisons;

E) Asking for finger snapping or hand clapping;

F) Utilizing any disturbance or occurrence at hand in the room;

G) Song by certain group or artist;

H) Do you feel like singing some more?;

J) Songs to whistle to.

A Day in the Life **[Cii]**
A Hard Day's Night **[B]**
After Midnight **[G]**
Bad Bad Leroy Brown **[H]**
Blue Suede Shoes **[A]**
Born To Be Wild **[Cvii]**
(On) Broadway
Chicago **[Cii]**
{Devil in the Blue Dress/Good Golly
Miss Molly/CC Ryder/Ginny Ginny/
Long Tall Sally Medley} **[A]**
Diana **[H]**
Do Wa Diddy **[AEH]**
Dock of the Bay **[C]**
Father and Son **[Cviii]**
Framed **[B]**
(The) Gay Caballero **[B]**
Great Balls of Fire **[D]**
Hava nagila**[Cii]**
{Heartbreak Hotel/Jailhouse Rock} **[A]**
{Hound Dog/Don't Be Cruel/Teddy
Bear} **[A]**
In the Kitchen **[F]**
It's Hard to be Humble **[B]**
King of the Road **[H]**

La Bamba/Twist & Shout **[A]**
Light My Fire **[G]**
Little Darlin' **[A]**
Love Potion No. 9 **[C]**
Mack the Knife **[E]**
MacNamera's Band **[E]**
Me & Bobby McGee **[Cii]**
Day Dream**[J]**
New York, New York **[C]**
New York State of Mind
Old Time Rock & Roll **[A]**
Penny Lane **[Cii]**
People Are Strange **[B]**
Pink Cadillac **[A]**
Rainy Day Woman #12 and 35 **[Cvi]**
Rebel Yell **[AGH]**
Rock & Roll Music **[A]**
Rock Around the Clock **[A]**
Rock This Town **[A]**
Runaround Sue **[B]**
Saturday Night **[A]**
Sea of Love **[Cv]**
{Splish Splash/At the Hop} **[A]**
Twist and Shout **[A]**
Twistin' the Night Away **[Cvii]**

22. Special Occasions:

A) Birthdays;

B) Anniversaries;

C) Hot date, wedding or honeymoon;

D) Full moon or weather phenomena;

E) Arriving or leaving town;

F) Meet someone or pick up night;

G) Holidays (Christmas, 4th of July, etc.);

H) Bar Room drinking or smoking song;

I) Employment: Hired or lost job;

J) Time of year (Seasons change, etc.);

K) Sad and lonely blues or break-up situation song.

Against All Odds [K]
Brandy [H]
Bring It On Home [F]
{Buddy Holly Medley: Oh Boy/Maybe
Baby/Peggy Sue/That Will Be the Day}
[K] Bye Bye Love [K]
Downtown [F]
Everybody's Talkin' At Me [F]
For the Longest Time [CF] -Game of
Love [F]
Great Balls of Fire [C]
Hello [BCF]
I Just Called to Say I Love You [BCF]
In the Kitchen [F]
Just the Way You Are [B]
Key Largo [K]
Lonely People [K]
Lookin' for Love [F]
Love on the Rocks [H]
MacNamera's Band [GH]
Maneater [F]
Margaritaville [H]
Moondance [D]
Moonshadow [D]
Raindrops [E]

Rainy Day Woman #12 and 35 [H]
Rebel Yell [C]
Right Here Waitin' For You [K]
Runaround Sue [K]
Satisfaction [K]
Sea of Love [BC]
(Whole Lot of) Shakin' [C]
Smoke Gets in Your Eyes [H]
Stand By Me [D]
Steppin' Out [F]
Stick With the Dogs [F]
Stuck On You [BCF]
Suddenly [F]
Suffragette City [E]
Summertime Blues [J]
Sunny [D]
Take This Job and Shove It [I]
Truly [BCF]
Twist and Shout [C]
Twistin' the Night Away [AH]
(The) Wanderer [F]
We Got To Get Out of This Place [E]
You Are [BCF]

23. City songs or songs from or about other countries

Allentown
Arthur's Theme
Bad Bad Leroy Brown
Born To Be Wild
California Girls
(On) Broadway
Chicago
City of New Orleans
Country Roads
Dock of the Bay
Georgia
I Am I Said

I Love L.A.
Kansas City
Kentucky Woman
Key Largo
La Bamba
Lukenback, Texas (Basics of Love)
MacNamera's Band
Margaritaville
New York, New York
Rainy Day Woman #12 and 35
Surfin' USA

24. Songs from movies or musicals

Against All Odds
Arthur's Theme
At This Moment
Chariots of Fire
Climb Every Mountain
Duelin' Banjos
Everybody's Talkin' At Me
Flashdance
Getting To Know You
Heartlight

It Might Be You
Lady In Red
Lookin' for Love
Memory (Theme from "Cats")
My Favorite Things
New York, New York
Oh, What a Beautiful Morning
Raindrops
You Are the Sunshine of My Life
You Light Up My Life

• NOTES •